Publications of the
CENTRE FOR REFORMATION AND RENAISSANCE STUDIES

GENERAL EDITOR William R. Bowen
ASSOCIATE EDITOR Joseph Black

Renaissance and Reformation Texts in Translation, 2

SERIES EDITOR Erika Rummel

Victoria University
in the
University of Toronto

Galateo

A Renaissance Treatise
on Manners

Giovanni Della Casa

Translated, with an Introduction and Notes, by
Konrad Eisenbichler and Kenneth R. Bartlett

3rd Edition, Revised

Toronto
Centre for Reformation and Renaissance Studies
1994

Canadian Cataloguing-in-Publication Data

Della Casa, Giovanni, 1503–1556
    Galateo: A Renaissance Treatise on Manners

(Renaissance and Reformation texts in translation; 2)
3rd ed. rev.
Translation of: Galateo.
Includes bibliographical references.
ISBN 0–9697512–2–2

1. Etiquette, Medieval (to 1600). 2. Conversation.
I. Eisenbichler, Konrad. II. Bartlett, Kenneth R., 1948– .
III. Victoria University (Toronto, Ont.). Centre for Reformation
and Renaissance Studies. IV. Title. V. Series.

BJ1921.D4513   1994   395   C94–930803–X

For distribution and information on the series write to:

CRRS Publications
Centre for Reformation and Renaissance Studies
Victoria University, University of Toronto
Toronto, Canada
M5S 1K7

Cover illustration: Agnolo Bronzino, *Portrait of a Man* c. 1550–55. By
permission of the National Gallery of Canada, Ottawa.

Printed in Canada.

Contents

Introduction

The Life of Giovanni Della Casa

Giovanni Della Casa was born in 1503 on the family estates in the Mugello, a mountainous region to the north-east of Florence. His father, Pandolfo, and his mother, Lisabetta Tornabuoni, belonged to the Florentine patriciate which had long been active in both politics and commerce. Della Casa's early childhood was spent in Rome, where his father resided on business, but he was soon sent to Florence for his education, studying with Ubaldino Bandinelli, whom he affectionately remembers in his *Galateo* (see p. 43, note 17).[1]

In 1525, Della Casa began the study of law at Bologna. There he also attended the lectures of the celebrated Latinist Romolo Amaseo and the Aristotelian philosopher Pietro Pomponazzi. His association with Renaissance humanist learning had begun. He became a close friend of Ludovico Beccadelli, with whom he retired to his villa in the Mugello for a year of intensive classical studies and immersion in Cicero's works (1525–26). Two years later, Della Casa travelled with Beccadelli to Padua to study Greek and thus further his humanistic studies. In Padua, whose university was the intellectual centre of the Venetian Republic, he became the friend of Pietro Bembo, one of the leaders of the Italian literary community.[2]

---

[1] On humanist education, see the still fundamental volume by William Harrison Woodward, *Studies in Education during the Age of the Renaissance, 1400–1600* (Cambridge: UP, 1906); see also his collection of humanist treatises on education entitled *Vittorino da Feltre and Other Humanist Educators* (Cambridge: UP, 1897; rpt. New York: Columbia University Teachers' College, 1963). More recently, see Paul Grendler, *Schooling in Renaissance Italy: Literacy and Learning, 1300–1600* (Baltimore: Johns Hopkins UP, 1989).

[2] Cardinal Pietro Bembo (1470–1547) is most important for his contribution to the debate on the Italian language (see p. 23). He was also a poet and literary

Della Casa himself had decided upon a literary career as a gentleman poet and *bon vivant*. In late 1528 he moved to Rome and wrote many witty, sophisticated—and often obscene—poems in the style of his friend and companion Francesco Berni.[3] At this time he composed a Latin treatise on marriage *(Lepidissima quaestio an uxor sit ducenda)*, which betrays his anti-feminism and misogyny, traits that occasionally resurface in *Galateo*. Together with the poets Francesco Berni, Agnolo Firenzuola and Francesco Maria Molza, he established the literary academy of the "vine-dressers" (Accademia de' Vignaiuoli), devoted, as its name suggests, to pleasure as well as to literature.[4]

During this period of dissipation and elegant, learned decadence (a phase of his life that later caused Della Casa considerable embarrassment) he came under the protection of the powerful Farnese family, attaching himself to the young Cardinal Alessandro Farnese, grandson of Pope Paul III (1534–49).[5]

While in Rome Della Casa decided to enter the church and pursue an ecclesiastical career, despite the fact that he lacked a true religious vocation. In so doing, he was following a common practice at the time, for young men of high rank and learning did see the Church as

theorist of note. He appears as a character in Baldassare Castiglione's *The Book of the Courtier*, where he expounds on the theories of platonic love.

[3] Francesco Berni (?1497–1535) gave his name to a type of lyric burlesque poetry *(bernesco)* that flourished in the Cinquecento. Born in Florence, he moved to Rome (1517) and entered the service first of Pope Leo X (Giovanni de' Medici), and then of Cardinal Bernardo Dovizi da Bibbiena (d. 1520). He later served Giovan Matteo Giberti, bishop of Verona (see p. 36 n.9). Berni died of poison at the house of Cardinal Innocenzo Cibo, apparently a victim of the power struggle between the two Medici heirs Alessandro and Ippolito.

[4] Agnolo Firenzuola (1493–1543) is best known for his 1548 treatise *On the Beauty of Women*, trans. Konrad Eisenbichler and Jacqueline Murray (Philadelphia: U of Pennsylvania P, 1992). Francesco Maria Molza (1489–1544) wrote elegant poetry in both Italian and Latin.

[5] The Farnese were a noble family, originally from Latium, with a long tradition of support for the papacy. They rose to prominence in Rome under Pope Alexander VI Borgia largely through Giulia Farnese's personal influence over the pope. In 1534 Alessandro Farnese was elected pope as Paul III. His son, Pierluigi (d. 1547), was elevated to the Duchy of Parma and Piacenza. Pierluigi's son, Ottavio, married the natural daughter of the Emperor Charles V. Cardinal Alessandro Farnese (d. 1589), brother of Ottavio, was the patron of Pietro Bembo.

a career. Della Casa was probably advised to choose this route to fortune and influence by his Farnese protectors who were able to advance him rapidly in the papal service. In 1537 Della Casa took holy orders and was soon after appointed a clerk of the Apostolic Camera, the finance department of the papacy. Given his wealth, education, wit, literary reputation, and high connections, his rise was rapid. In 1538 he was given the honorific title of Monsignor; and three years later he received his first diplomatic appointment as a papal collector in Florence.[6] While there (1541–43), he entered the intellectual life of the Medicean capital and took a very active part in the proceedings of the newly formed Accademia Fiorentina.[7]

In 1544 Della Casa was named Archbishop of Benevento and papal nuncio to Venice.[8] The last was an extremely delicate position because he had not only to deal with the jealously guarded traditional independence of the Serenissima in ecclesiastical affairs but also to administer and implement the decisions emanating from the Council of Trent for the reformation of the Roman church. In 1547 he was responsible for the establishment of the Venetian Inquisition, the *Tre savi sopra eresia*.[9] Between 1545–49 he also conducted the heresy proceedings against Pier Paolo Vergerio the Younger, Bishop of Capodistria, who took the opportunity to attack the nuncio for his earlier licentious life in Rome.[10] At this time Della Casa composed two brilliantly argued political and diplo-

---

[6]Papal collectors were officers charged with receiving taxes, fees and dues owed to the papacy.

[7]Founded in 1540 under the name of Accademia degli Umidi (Academy of the Wet Ones), it quickly attracted grand-ducal interest and patronage. This led the Academy to change its name to Accademia Fiorentina (1541) and thus become an official, state-sponsored organ of Florentine intellectual life. The Academy met to discuss literature and language with an aim to promote the Tuscan literary and linguistic tradition. Some of the most important thinkers and literati of contemporary Florence belonged to the Academy.

[8]A nuncio is an ambassador representing the Holy See.

[9]Since the thirteenth century, heresy in Venice had been the jurisdiction of a secular magistracy. In 1541 a new magistracy, the *savi*, was instituted to deal with specific charges of heresy before the Venetian courts.

[10]On Pier Paolo Vergerio, see Anne Jacobson Schutte, *Pier Paolo Vergerio: The Making of an Italian Reformer* (Geneva: Droz, 1977); and Antonio Santossuoso, "Religion *More Veneto* and the Trial of Pier Paolo Vergerio," in *Peter Martyr Vermigli and Italian Reform*, ed. J.C. McLelland (Waterloo, ON: Wilfrid Laurier UP, 1980), 43–61.

matic orations in which his political acumen and views are revealed: the *Oration to the Emperor Charles v for the Restitution of Piacenza* (1548) and the *Oration to Exhort the Venetian Republic to Join in League with the Pope and the King of France against the Emperor Charles v* (1548). These views, such as his hostility to the Spaniards then dominating much of the peninsula, subsequently recur in *Galateo*. Similarly, his Latin treatise on office-holding *(De officiis inter potentiores et tenuiores amicos*, later translated into Italian by Della Casa or by his nephew, Annibale Rucellai, and into English by Henry Stubbe as *The Arts of Grandeur and Submission)* introduces a number of the major themes of *Galateo*.[11]

In 1548 Della Casa returned to Rome where he was largely responsible for the compilation of the Index of Prohibited Books.[12] The following year, however, his fortunes collapsed: his patron Pope Paul III Farnese died and Cardinal Giovanni Maria Del Monte, who was hostile to the Farnese and their dependents, was elected to the See of St. Peter (Julius III, reigned 1550–55). Consequently, Della Casa lost both his position of influence in Rome and his nunciature in Venice. He therefore decided to retire to private life and relative tranquillity in the Venetian Republic. His chosen place of repose was the abbey of Nervesa, on the slopes of the Montello in the March of Treviso, far from the cares and responsibilities of papal diplomacy. During these years (1552–55) Della Casa wrote the *Galateo* and composed some of his best poetry.

With the accession of Pope Paul IV Carafa (1555), Della Casa's fortunes improved once again.[13] He was recalled to Rome and named Secretary of State.[14] Notwithstanding this high office, Della Casa was

---

[11]Santossuoso dates this work after 1537 and before 1543; see his *Vita di Giovanni Della Casa*, p. 72.

[12]The success of the Lutherans in harnessing the power of the printing press drove Roman Catholics to attempt to control the proliferation of heterodox titles. This process began in the late 1540s under Della Casa. In 1559 Pope Paul IV Carafa introduced the first official Roman Index of Prohibited Books, which included not only the works of reformers but also those of Erasmus, all vernacular Bibles, and the titles printed by 61 printers.

[13]Gian Pietro Carafa (1476–1559) enjoyed a well-earned reputation for severity. His determined pursuit and punishment of heretical thinkers is perhaps best illustrated by his alleged claim that "If my father were a heretic, I myself would gather the wood to burn him at the stake."

[14]The Secretary of State, or *Secretarius maior*, was established by Pope Leo X

bitterly disappointed at not being included in Paul IV's first list of elevations to the Sacred College. Disillusioned and prematurely aged, Giovanni Della Casa died in Rome in November 1556.

The Italian Context of *Galateo*

The life of Giovanni Della Casa coincided with one of the most cataclysmic periods in the history of the Italian people and the Roman church. In 1494 King Charles VIII of France invaded Italy and began a series of foreign interventions into the peninsula that resulted in Italy becoming the battlefield of Europe, the theatre in which the competing claims of the French Valois and the Spanish-Imperial Hapsburgs for hegemony over the continent were largely decided.[15] Between 1494 and 1529 virtually continuous warfare shattered the Italian peninsula, devastating states, families, economies, and institutions. The great battles of Italy—Agnadello (1509), Marignano (1515), Pavia (1525)—indicated clearly that Italians could no longer defend their country and that the future of Italy would be decided beyond the Alps.

Some measure of peace returned to Italy after 1529, when the Hapsburgs had effectively crushed French ambitions in the peninsula and emerged as the dominant power in Italian affairs. However, such peace was achieved only after one of the most brutal events of a brutal time: the Sack of Rome in 1527 by rioting Spanish and German Imperial troops. The horror and barbarism of this act had few analogues in history to that time, and the memory of the atrocities committed had a profound effect upon the Italian imagination.[16]

The events of the first half of the century had equally profound effects on Della Casa's native Florence. The 1494 invasion had resulted in the expulsion of the Medici family from Florence and the reestablishment of a broadly based Republic. In 1512 the Medici, sup-

---

in 1513 within the Apostolic Secretariat. The significance of this office was that it directed papal correspondence in the vernacular, a role that grew in responsibility until it overshadowed the traditional positions in the papal secretariat. Under Paul III in particular the office was an important appointment in the curia.

[15]For a contemporary view, see Francesco Guicciardini, *The History of Italy*, trans. S. Alexander (New York: Macmillan, 1969).

[16]See Judith Hook, *The Sack of Rome, 1527* (New York: Macmillan, 1972) and André Chastel, *The Sack of Rome, 1527* (Princeton: Princeton UP, 1983).

ported by Spanish troops, regained the city and were returned to power. The following year Giovanni de' Medici was elected pope (Leo x) and ruled the city through his cousin, Cardinal Giulio de' Medici. In 1527, however, the republican traditions of the Florentines were rekindled by the Sack of Rome and the Medici were again driven from Florence. The catastrophies of that year made impossible any assault on this last Florentine Republic by the current Medici pope (Giulio de' Medici, now Pope Clement vii). But in 1529, after Clement vii had made peace with the Hapsburg Emperor Charles v, an Imperial army composed of Spanish and German soldiers laid siege to Florence and finally captured it in August of 1530. The Medici were again returned to power in the city and again owed their rehabilitation to Spanish arms. The Republic of Florence ended forever when Alessandro de' Medici, purported to be the illegitimate son of Pope Clement vii, was appointed Duke of Florence by the Emperor Charles v. The accession of Cosimo I de' Medici as Duke of Florence in 1537 completed the process of turning Florence into a hereditary Medici duchy (and later, in 1559, into a grand-duchy). Cosimo I, though still largely dependent upon the Spanish garrison in his city, destroyed the last vestiges of the old republican system, took a Spanish wife and turned Tuscany into an absolute monarchy.[17]

By 1540, then, the Spaniards were supreme in Italy, ruling Naples, Sicily, Milan, Sardinia, and enjoying Tuscany (where they controlled five important fortresses) and Genoa virtually as dependent states. The States of the Church had not yet recovered from the Sack of Rome and the pope needed peace with the triumphant Spaniards. In all Italy, only Venice maintained her independence, although even the Serenissima was circumspect after its devastating defeat at Agnadello (1509).[18]

This was the political and diplomatic context of Della Casa's life and of the *Galateo*. Italy, her people and states, had suffered constant humiliation at the hands of foreign "barbarians" (to use Machiavelli's term). Fortune had apparently deserted her and her fate was in the

---

[17]For a description of the 1530 capitulation to the Spanish, the 1537 assassination of Duke Alessandro and Cosimo I's immediate accession to power, see Eric Cochrane, *Florence in the Forgotten Centuries 1527–1800* (Chicago: U of Chicago P, 1973), 1–92.

[18]See D.S. Chambers, *The Imperial Age of Venice, 1380–1580* (London: Thames and Hudson, 1970).

hands of others. Her culture, though despoiled and dislocated, still excited the envy of Europe, and so did her riches. To a patrician Florentine like Della Casa, scion of the old Republic, the vision was terrible. It is indeed possible that his dissipated life during the years 1528–37 was in part a reaction to these truths. Similarly, there can be no doubt but that the *Galateo*, like Baldassare Castiglione's *Book of the Courtier*, represented a response to the sense of helplessness occasioned by the events of his youth and what they had done to his native land.

The spiritual world of Catholicism was also irrevocably shattered during Della Casa's lifetime. Martin Luther's publication of his 95 theses in 1517 had begun the dissolution of the universal Church. Luther was soon followed by others: John Calvin, Huldrich Zwingli, and even Henry VIII of England who withdrew his nation from the Roman confession. Italy itself witnessed the stirrings of reform and the very foundations of the world into which Della Casa had been born were collapsing.

In the face of this fragmentation of the Church, there arose Roman Catholics who wished to confront the successes of the Protestant Reformation. In 1540, Pope Paul III Farnese, Della Casa's patron, approved the formation of the Society of Jesus (the Jesuits) as organized by St. Ignatius of Loyola (1491–1556).[19] This new order, schooled by its founder's *Spiritual Exercises*,[20] injected a rigid and disciplined code of behaviour into the Church. Also, by adopting elements of rationalist, humanistic teaching, a vocation for education, and a special concern for the established powers of the secular world, the Jesuits provided an effective opposition to the further spread of the Reformation.

Moreover, a group of reforming high clerics, including powerful cardinals such as Pietro Carafa (1476–1559), Gasparo Contarini (1483–1542), Reginald Pole (1500–58), and others, saw a real need for Rome to address some of the abuses identified by Luther, Calvin, and their followers. After false starts beginning in 1537, a great council for the reform of the Church met in 1545 in Trent, in northern

---

[19] For the Jesuits, see T.J. Campbell, *The Jesuits* (New York, 1921); and John W. O'Malley, *The First Jesuits* (Cambridge, MA: Harvard, 1993).

[20] See H. Rahner, *The Spirituality of St. Ignatius Loyola* (Westminster, MD: Newman Press, 1953).

Italy, to begin the difficult task of redefining or reconfirming the teachings and the institutions of Catholicism. On and off for eighteen years (1545–63), the Council of Trent met and succeeded in re- animating the besieged Church.[21]

The proceedings of Trent also helped define Della Casa's world view. New rules, new doctrines, or old ones reinforced, flowed from the Council. Intellectual weapons to combat heresy emerged, such as the reconstituted Inquisitions established at Rome and by Della Casa himself at Venice, and the Index of Prohibited Books on which he diligently worked. These procedures and this atmosphere found their way into *Galateo,* making it a digest of the values of its age.

Having lived through the devastation and dislocation of his native land and his Church, having witnessed the humiliation of popes, kings, princes and republics, and having observed the transitory nature of power and glory, Della Casa was perhaps offering a small remedy in his *Galateo.* Order, precedence, manners and rules provide structure both to societies and to an individual's life. In the chaos of the first half of the sixteenth century, the lessons of *Galateo* could offer comfort and useful advice, allowing each man the opportunity to improve his own immediate world, to cultivate his own garden.

Galateo

Courtesy books have a special relationship to the age which produces them. By attempting to codify the manners, styles, ideals and values of a society, the author reveals the principles and presuppositions that shape and animate his world. For this reason, books of manners or deportment should not be relegated to the studies of antiquarians or ransacked to provide the collections of exempla that illustrate popular history. Rather, courtesy books should be used critically as a means of discovering the *mentalité* of an epoch quickly and effectively: they provide an entry into the complex social and intellectual structures of the past.

The *Galateo* does this brilliantly. It reflects the personal experience, wisdom, disappointments, and ambitions of its clerical but worldly wise author. It also reflects the fundamental values of his age. And, given that his age was one of transformation, from the High Renaissance

---

[21]The standard work on the Council of Trent is Hubert Jedin's *A History of the Council of Trent,* 2 vols. (St. Louis: B. Herder, 1957–1961).

in Italy to the world of the Counter-Reformation, and that Della Casa was an important actor in the events of his time, the lessons are particularly valuable and worth considering at some length.

Courtesy books in general and the *Galateo* in particular have illustrious antecedents. Della Casa's humanistic education would have made him familiar with the *Nicomachean Ethics* of Aristotle (384–322 B.C.), with the *Characters of Men* by Theophrastus (*c.*372–287 B.C.), the *Moralia* of Plutarch (*c.*46–*c.*120 A.D.), and especially with the many extant works of the Roman politician, orator, and strict moralist Tullius Cicero (106–43 B.C.). These classical authors provided much of the genesis of the modern courtesy book and many of their fundamental ideas. They dealt with principles, most significantly with those principles that determined human interaction: man was a social animal and his society required certain codes of behaviour to lubricate its operation. And these are also the lessons of the *Galateo*.

More immediately, Della Casa would have known those modern texts of manners which shared these assumptions: Paolo da Certaldo's *Book of Manners* (*Il libro dei costumi*), Pier Paolo Vergerio the Elder's *On Conduct Worthy of Free Men* (*De ingenuis moribus*) and Jacopo Sadoleto's *On the Correct Education of Children* (*De liberis recte instituendis*). And, most especially, there was the towering monument to the age, Baldassare Castiglione's *The Book of the Courtier*. What all such books have in common is the belief that men can improve themselves, that human beings naturally desire to subscribe to an ideal and that the ideal is attainable. Also, there is the assumption that external manners are expressions and manifestations of internal qualities: good men exhibit good manners.[22]

Because of its importance and the importance of the age in which it was written, the *Galateo* provides a useful illustration of this truth. Della Casa, born of a Florentine patrician family with strong republican credentials, represented in himself and in his own education a set of values and principles which rest just below the surface of the *Galateo*. First, he assumes the reader will be a public person, a man active in the world.[23] By the early sixteenth century, the old medieval debate

---

[22] For further information on courtesy books in the Renaissance, see *Etiquette et Politesse*, ed. Alain Montandon (Clermont-Ferrand, 1992) and *Traités de Savoir-vivre en Italie*, ed. Alain Montandon (Clermont-Ferrand, 1992).

[23] The treatise is addressed to men, and not to women. Sixteenth-century Italian

between the contemplative and the active life, still so powerful in Petrarch (d. 1374) and in Coluccio Salutati (d. 1406), was over. By the time of Leonardo Bruni (d. 1444), Florentines in particular had become convinced that true human dignity comes from service to one's fellow citizens and service to the state. Individual growth was made possible by social intercourse and political activity; men of culture and learning were needed to serve the state and their education reflected this expectation.[24]

Eloquence, wisdom, knowledge and good judgment came from a humanist education in classical studies. Those who best displayed and applied that education and its fruits became the leaders of their societies and the examples for future generations. Hence, how one behaved, how one spoke, how one dressed and how one learned contributed to one's image, one's public personality, which was seen not as a superficial veneer but as an expression of the inner self. Thus, the quest for *virtù*, or individual prowess, resourcefulness, and capability, predetermined the cult of the *virtuoso*. In the *Galateo* Della Casa is offering advice on achieving virtuosity and all the obvious and unstated perquisites and responsibilities which attend it.

Despite (or perhaps because of) Della Casa's own ecclesiastical career, he does not privilege the contemplative over the active life. There is no suggestion in his treatise that a life devoted to contemplation may be an equally meritorious pursuit for a gentleman of education and manners. His cultural background and his experience of contemporary political and religious questions had convinced him, instead, that the active live was preferable. He thus followed in the path of Florentine humanists of the Quattrocento who had rejected the essentially medieval notion of the superiority of the contemplative life, and obeyed the imperatives of the Counter-Reformation which made active involvement in the world so much more necessary, both for lay and clerical Catholics.[25]

----

culture gave women an important role to play within the family, but did not really allow them a part in the civic or public life of their society.

[24]G. Griffiths, J. Hankins, D. Thompson, *The Humanism of Leonardo Bruni: Selected Texts* (Binghamton, NY: MRTS, 1987); Hans Baron, *The Crisis of the Early Italian Renaissance* (Princeton, NJ: Princeton UP, 1955).

[25]For a Quattrocento discussion on this topic, see Lorenzo Valla's *On the Profession of the Religious ...*, trans. Olga Pugliese, 2nd ed. (Toronto: CRRS, 1994).

Therefore, Della Casa can be compared in some ways as much with Machiavelli (1469–1527), his fellow Florentine republican patrician, as with Castiglione (1478–1529). Machiavelli and Della Casa were the product of the same traditions: humanism, republicanism, and the Florentine *vita civile*, or active life. Machiavelli codified the cult of *virtù* in his description of the ideal prince. Indeed, *The Prince* is not unlike a book of manners for a new or aspiring ruler. The ideal is attainable and the means of achieving it are rational and discernable; once acquired, the effects for both the prince, the man of *virtù*, and his state, his society, will be positive and redeeming. Foreign models and foreign masters are to be avoided and ultimately overcome so that finally Italy and its people might be liberated and again worthy of republicanism.[26]

Della Casa teaches many of the same lessons. He, too, offers advice for the acquisition of *virtù*. He counsels against foreign styles and manners, and particularly against imitation of Spanish customs and manners. And, above all, he provides precepts for success in the world based not upon abstract principles but upon experience. Like Machiavelli, Della Casa uses experience and concrete examples to instruct the reader in the way to achieve both personal and social success. Machiavelli and Della Casa, then, have much in common. It is not surprising, therefore, that the first recorded justification of dire measures "for reasons of state" ("ragion di stato") appears not in Machiavelli but in Della Casa.

In *The Book of the Courtier* Castiglione also assumes the existence of an ideal and the perfectibility of man.[27] He, too, is concerned with the external manifestations of those qualities and he writes from per-

---

[26]The bibliography on Machiavelli is vast. A starting point for the general student may be the Norton Critical Edition of *The Prince*, trans. and ed. Robert M. Adams (New York and London: W.W. Norton, 1977), which contains not only a translation of the text, with notes and introduction, but also selections from Machiavelli's other writings and from studies on Machiavelli by other scholars. See also *Niccolò Machiavelli. An Annotated Bibliography of Modern Criticism and Scholarship*, ed. S. Ruffo-Fiore (Greenwood, 1992).

[27]The bibliography on Castiglione is also vast. One could start with J.R. Woodhouse, *Baldesar Castiglione. A Reassessment of "The Courtier'* (Edinburgh: Edinburgh UP, 1978) and with the collection of essays entitled *Castiglione. The Ideal and the Real in Renaissance Culture*, ed. Robert W. Hanning and David Rosand (New Haven and London: Yale UP, 1983).

sonal, if nostalgically idealized, experience. However, Castiglione dif-
fers from Machiavelli and Della Casa in a fundamental way. He teaches
that man's best hope for realizing his ideals resides in service to a
prince. He is far more philosophical than Della Casa and far more
dependent on the elitist and ultimately exclusive Neoplatonism of the
later Renaissance. Because Castiglione wished for a renovation of the
interior man, not for a newly active social structure, he occasionally
seems almost to owe more to the ideals of the old writers on the contemplative life. His ideals are abstract and distant, and dependent not
so much on the relations among men as upon the individual's climb-
ing of the Platonic ladder of perfection and upon the relationship
between the nobly born courtier and his prince, and ultimately,
between the rarefied spirit and God.[28]

Della Casa makes other assumptions, again largely based upon his
humanist training coloured, however, by the cataclysmic events of the
first decades of the sixteenth century. For Della Casa, a necessary
quality for success is the Horatian golden mean (*aurea mediocritas*),
the classical ideal of a middle road between excesses. This principle is
reinforced by that Florentine virtue of good sense, based upon
informed observation, which helps to determine the appropriateness
of all things, depending on their circumstances. Thus, despite his
explicit injunctions against vice and against evil behaviour, there is little in the *Galateo* that is absolute. Della Casa's world is the real world
of complex situations and mitigating circumstances: he always deals
with man in his social context, avoiding moral commandments that
might not be appropriate in every case.

He is a formulator of general but not inviolate rules, an observer of
the world who wishes to codify its lessons as far as possible in order to
assist those who are less experienced in dealing with the difficulties
inherent in human affairs. In short, Della Casa is a teacher; and the
Galateo is his text. Much of his method comes from the intellectual
climate of the age, a period when behaviour was closely monitored,
corrected, or punished. Such activities betray a desire for order, structure and rules. Follow the rules and you will be accepted, even rewarded;
break the rules and you will be suspected, perhaps even condemned.

---

[28]See G. Pico della Mirandola, *Oration on the Dignity of Man,* in *The Renaissance Philosophy of Man,* ed. E. Cassirer, P.O. Kristeller, J.H. Randall (Chicago:
U of Chicago P, 1948, 1969), 223–56.

In this context the *Galateo* may be compared with the *Spiritual Exercises* of Ignatius of Loyola insofar as both are teaching manuals; one for men as social animals, the other for men as spiritual beings.

There is, then, a significant contribution from the Counter-Reformation to Della Casa's method, if not to his message. Strive towards the ideal but do so only according to the accepted rules of order. A fundamen-tal purpose of the *Galateo* is to teach its reader how to be recognized as part of the dominant, controlling culture of one's society. Proper, measured and polished behaviour is not only aesthetically pleasing and socially useful but is also a caste mark indicating membership in the powerful elite. In this way, Della Casa is suggesting that social mobility is possible, though not easy. The social structure of mid-sixteenth century Italy was solidifying into virtually closed castes. Nevertheless, as a humanist, Della Casa is also implying the existence of a nobility of virtue, visible through its deeds, that parallels, if not supersedes, nobility of birth. Here again, Della Casa illustrates how the values of one age still in-form the next, how the humanism of Quattrocento Florence retained some of its vigour and its ideals, even in the age of the Council of Trent.

The Narrator and the Language

The *Galateo* springs from the private desire of a middle-aged man, once influential in affairs, to advise a younger member of his family in the ways of the world. The idea for such a work was first suggested to Della Casa during his residence in Rome by Galeazzo Florimonte, Bishop of Sessa. In the introduction to the 1558 *editio princeps,* Erasmo Gemini de Cessis, Della Casa's secretary (and the man responsible for saving the *Galateo* by convincing Della Casa's heirs to allow it to be published), recalls the event in vivid terms: the bishop mentioned the need for such a book, flattered Della Casa by praising his literary abilities, and offered to assist him in writing it by illustrating the manners he himself had found most praiseworthy while a guest of Giovanni Matteo Giberti, the Bishop of Verona (see p. 36 n. 9).

Della Casa agreed to respond to Florimonte's invitation. The result was *De officiis inter potentiores et tenuiores amicos* (1546). This treatise on the relationship between friends of differing social classes was soon translated into Italian (1559). Translations into French followed in 1571 by Gervias Mallot and in 1648 by Guillaume Colletet. The first

English translation, under the title *The Arts of Grandeur and Submission*, is by Henry Stubbe (1665).[29] Della Casa's first attempt at writing a book of manners was largely a failure. Heavily indebted to Cicero's *De officiis,* Della Casa's text is too pedantic, derivative and literary to be successful.

After his retirement from the taxing political worlds of Tridentine Rome and Venice, however, Della Casa addressed the subject of good social manners once again. On this occasion, the repose he enjoyed in the pleasant surroundings of the March of Treviso transformed the style and structure of his work. Della Casa significantly changed the tone and intent of the book by introducing the narrator figure of an unlearned old man, an *idiota* (one who is not an expert, in the original Greek meaning), who relies on his own experience rather than on books to reveal his subject. This technique permits the effective blend of narrative levels that gives the work variety and vitality. At one moment the narrator is self-consciously "learned" (in the opening chapter, for example, with its complex sentence structure and ponderous, pedantic beginning), and at other times he forgets himself and refers familiarly to "some man by the name of Socrates' and his friend, "another good man who was called Aristophanes." The unlearned old man also often confuses his classical details and forgets names that Della Casa would undoubtedly have known. Nevertheless, his advice re-mains convincing and appropriate because it is clearly grounded in the realities of daily life, a far more effective foundation than classical learning.

The presence of the *idiota* narrator leads to two important considerations. First, it suggests that the subject matter of the *Galateo* is to be seen not as the exclusive right of the learned but as the common property of all men: the manners and style reflected in the book can be acquired and practised by anyone, though a gentleman born of a good family and with access to leisure time and the necessary amount of wealth would of course find the regimen more useful and easier to follow. Second, the matter discussed can be learned from experience and from daily life much more easily and far better than from books. The implied reference to Castiglione's elegant and learned coterie assembled in Urbino and described in *The Book of the Courtier* is self-evident.

---

[29]See Antonio Santosuosso, "Books, Readers, and Critics. The Case of Giovanni Della Casa, 1537–1975," *La Bibliofilia* 79 (1977), 104–05.

The narrator figure, then, is not an image of Della Casa, the humanist with a complete classical education. Nevertheless, Della Casa's refined culture, extensive learning and consummate experience in the world of high society are built into the structure and meaning of the text. The references and borrowings from Cicero, Aristotle, and other classical writers are numerous. So are questions of contemporary concern, such as the presence and influence of the Spanish in Italy, or the "questione della lingua," the lively debate then being carried out across the peninsula by almost every major writer in Italy on the nature and standards of what ought to be the official Italian language.[30]

By the Cinquecento, renewed interest in Italian as a literary, scientific and national idiom had given rise to a debate on language that was to last the entire century. The Venetian writer Pietro Bembo, whom Della Casa had met and befriended during his years in Padua (1528–29), had proposed a purely literary language based on the works of Petrarch for poetry and Boccaccio for prose. Imitation of the vocabulary and style of the two fourteenth-century Florentine writers was seen by Bembo and the *bembisti* as the ultimate expression of a universal Italian language. In response to this restrictive, erudite proposal, some writers (Machiavelli among them) strongly argued that language is a living entity, constantly changing and adapting itself to different needs. They thus proposed that contemporary spoken Florentine should be the ideal Italian idiom. A middle ground between Bembo's closed proposal and the open, fluid Florentine concept was advanced by writers such as Baldassare Castiglione and Ludovico Ariosto (1474–1533) who proposed, as Dante had done two centuries earlier in his *On the Vernacular Tongue* (*De vulgari eloquentia*), a language that reflected the general usage found in Italian courts and chanceries, an educated and elegant idiom which rose above local common speech to transcend regional boundaries and to unite the Italian linguistic community.[31]

In the *Galateo*, Della Casa shows himself to be fully aware of this

---

[30]For an introduction to the Question of the Language see Robert J. Hall, Jr., *The Italian Questione della Lingua: An Interpretative Essay* (Chapel Hill: U of North Carolina P, 1942); or Bruno Migliorini, *The Italian Language* (New York: Barnes & Noble, 1966).

[31]Dante's unfinished treatise on language is dated shortly after 1304. It surveys contemporary Italian dialects and then proposes the creation of a standard

debate. Much attention is devoted to the question of language (chapters 21–23), both in general, theoretical terms and in detailed, particular examples. Siding with Bembo and the purists, Della Casa finds Dante's harsh idiom inelegant, and contemporary Florentine (or any other local dialect) unsuitable. Equally, however, he admits that the language of Boccaccio and Petrarch has been superseded. The old narrator is thus made to speak in a contemporary idiom about contemporary matters, though the old man does try to elevate his language by emulating Boccaccio's style and by making classical allusions. For example, the opening paragraph is a fine example of the classical exordium (exhibiting much linguistic pedantry) in which the author presents and defends the argument he is about to develop. As a whole, however, the *Galateo* achieves a middle ground in which both Della Casa and his narrator illustrate the position developed by Ariosto in the attempt to fix a truly national idiom. As a result, in subsequent years Italian scholars came to look upon the *Galateo* not only as a document of its times or as the first book of its kind but also as one of the finest and most elegant examples of Renaissance Italian prose writing, worthy of linguistic study and emulation.

The Title of the Book

The title of the book is brilliantly allusive and illustrates the subtlety of Della Casa's mind. On the simplest level, it is derived from the Latinized form of Bishop Galeazzo Florimonte's name, *Galatheus* (see p. 37 n. 11). By naming his book on manners after the learned bishop, Della Casa was acknowledging Florimonte's contribution to the work (see above, p. 21). Galateo is also the masculine form of Galatea, the name given to the statue sculpted and loved by Pygmalion and then brought to life by the goddess Aphrodite.[32] This allusion not only represents the purpose of the book—the search for human ideals and the means of animating those ideals through fulfilling the potential in all

Italian for writing both poetry and prose. It also argues for the ability and flexibility of this standard Italian to discuss all subjects, be they philosophical, theological, narrative or poetic. See Marianne Shapiro, *De vulgari eloquentia: Dante's Book of Exile* (Lincoln: U of Nebraska P, 1990) for a modern English translation of the treatise, a discussion, and bibliography.

[32]Ovid, *Metamorphoses* 10.242–97.

men—but also provides a narrative coherence by linking the example of the painter Zeuxis of Heraclea given in chapter 26 to Galeazzo Florimonte and the title. In addition, Galatea is the name of the beautiful sea nymph who fled from the brutish giant Polyphemus, her unwanted suitor.[33] Raphael depicted this myth—again, almost an iconographical representation of Della Casa's theme—in the Sala di Galatea in the Farnesina palace in Rome (executed for the Sienese banker Agostino Chigi and finished in 1513). Della Casa would certainly have known the fresco which is among Raphael's most famous works.

The Translation

In this translation we have tried to retain the flavour of Della Casa's prose. The highly structured first chapter, with its ponderous, pedantic beginning, has been kept as complex as the original. Similarly, when Della Casa chose to use strong stylistic devices we sought to retain them in the English version as well. In most other cases, however, the long Italian periodic structure has been broken down to accommodate the shorter sentences of English prose. In the process we have not deleted any phrases or passages from Della Casa's original. This point, in fact, is one of the major differences between our translation and that made by the *Galateo*'s only other modern translator, R.S. Pine-Coffin (1950); at times Pine-Coffin's text becomes a paraphrase rather than a translation because it omits phrases which were obviously felt to be a burden to English prose.

The Pine-Coffin translation, it must be noted, was the first to have been done from the Italian original. Earlier English renditions had not been reliable: Robert Peterson's translation (1576) is based on the anonymous 1573 French version; the 1701 translation by "several young gentlemen educated at a private grammar school near Hackney" is not very accurate; the anonymous 1703 translation is a rather free rendition of the Latin version by Nathan Chytraeus; and Richard Graves, who did use the original Italian text, made so many alterations to it that he himself called his 1774 version a paraphrase. In short, until now there has not been available in English an accurate and complete rendition of Della Casa's *Galateo*.

---

[33] Ovid, *Metamorphoses* 13.750–897.

Bibliography

The translation is based on the standard Italian texts.

Il Galateo. Ed. Carlo Steiner. Milan: Francesco Vallardi, 1910.

Galateo ovvero de' costumi. Ed. Dino Provenzal. Milan: Rizzoli Editore, 1950.

Il Galateo. In *Prose di Giovanni della Casa e altri trattatisti cinquecenteschi del comportamento*, ed. Arnaldo di Benedetto, 191–263. Torino: U.T.E.T., 1979.

English Translations

Galateo of Maister Iohn Della Casa, Archebishop of Beneuenta. Or rather, A treatise of the Maners and behauiours, it behoueth a man to vse and eschewe, in his familiar conuersation. A worke very necessary & profitable for all Gentlemen, or other. Trans. Robert Peterson. London, 1576: rpt. New York: Da Capo, 1969.

Galateo: Or, a Treatise on Politeness and Delicacy of Manners. Trans. Richard Graves. London, 1774.

Galateo or The Book of Manners. Trans. R.S. Pine-Coffin. Harmondsworth, Middlesex: Penguin, 1958.

Works of Criticism

Falvo, Giuseppe. "Il *Galateo* e le *Rime* di Giovanni Della Casa." *Italian Culture* 9 (1991): 129–38.

Pine-Coffin, R.S. Introduction to *Galateo or The Book of Manners*. Harmondsworth, Middlesex: Penguin, 1958.

Pirotti, Umberto. "Il Della Casa del Galateo." *Studi e Problemi di Critica Testuale* 10 (1979): 29–56.

Prosperi, Gianluca. "Per una lettura antropologica del *Galateo* di Della Casa." *Studium* 73:3 (1980): 379–86.

Santosuosso, Antonio. *The Bibliography of Giovanni Della Casa: Books, Readers and Critics 1537–1975*. Florence: Olschki, 1979.

————. *Vita di Giovanni Della Casa*. Rome: Bulzoni, 1978.

————. "Life and Thought of Giovanni Della Casa, 1503–1556." PhD diss., University of Toronto, 1972.

————. "Giovanni Della Casa and His *Galateo*: On Life and Success in the Late Italian Renaissance." *Renaissance and Reformation* 11:1 (1975): 1–13.

————. "Books, Readers, and Critics. The Case of Giovanni Della Casa, 1537–1975." *La Bibliofilia* 79 (1977): 100–86.

————. "The Moderate Inquisitor. Giovanni Della Casa's Venetian Nunciature, 1544–1549." *Studi Veneziani*, n.s. 2 (1978): 119–210.

————. "Religion *More Veneto* and the Trial of Pier Paolo Vergerio." In *Peter Martyr Vermigli and Italian Reform*, ed. J.C. McLelland, 43–61. Waterloo, ON: Wilfrid Laurier UP, 1980.

Other Courtesy Books

Anon. *The Institucion of a Gentleman*. London, 1555; rpt. New York: Da Capo, 1974.

Brathwait, Richard. *The English Gentleman*. London, 1630; rpt. New York: Da Capo, 1975.

————. *The English Gentlewoman*. London, 1631; rpt. New York: Da Capo, 1970.

Castiglione, Baldassare. *The Book of the Courtier*. Trans. Charles S. Singleton. New York: Anchor Books, 1959.

Faret, Nicolas. *L'honneste-homme; ou, L'art de plaire a la court*. Paris, 1632.

Guazzo, Stefano. *Civile Conversation*. Trans. George Pettie (1581). London: Constable, 1925.

Le Grand, Jacques. *Boke of Curtesye*. Trans. William Caxton (1477–78). Ed. F.J. Furnivall. London, 1868; rpt. New York: Kraus, 1975.

Mancini, Domenico. *The Myrrour of Good Maners*. Trans. Alexander Barclay. London, [1518?].

Peacham, Henry. *The Complete Gentleman* (1622). Ed. V.B. Heltzel. Ithaca: Cornell UP, 1962.

Romei, Annibale. *The Courtier's Academie*. Trans. John Kepers. London, 1598; rpt. New York: Da Capo, 1969.

A Treatise
which, under the guise of an uneducated old man
instructing a young relative,
speaks of the manners to be observed or avoided
in dealing with society, and is entitled

Galateo,
or About Manners

Galateo, or About Manners

[1]

In as much as[1] you are now just starting that journey that is this earthly life which I, as you can see, have for the most part completed, and because I love you as much as I do, I have taken it upon myself to show you (as someone who has had experience) those places in which I fear you may easily either fail or fall, as you proceed through them, so that, if you follow my advice, you may stay on the right path towards the salvation of your soul as well as for the praise and honour of your distinguished and noble family.[2] And since your tender age would not be capable of grasping more important or subtle teachings, I will save them for a more suitable time and start with what many others might perhaps consider frivolous, that is, how I believe one ought to behave when speaking or dealing with other people so as to

---

[1] The opening preposition, "Con cio sia cosa che," is one of the most famous—or infamous—in Italian letters. The tragedian Vittorio Alfieri (1749–1803) claimed that, on reading these words, he tossed the book out the window in disgust. In beginning the treatise with such pomposity, Della Casa's intention was not, however, to lose his reader, but rather to help create the persona of the *idiota* narrator who strives for a learned effect but achieves, instead, pedantic academic affectation. For the narrative frame and the *idiota* topos, see the Introduction, pp. 22–23.

[2] The individual to whom the treatise is addressed is most probably Annibale Rucellai, Della Casa's nephew, and the son of his sister Dianora and Luigi Rucellai. The Rucellai were an ancient and prominent family of Florence, active in Florentine affairs from at least the thirteenth century. At the end of that century, they participated in the restructuring of the commune to exclude the magnates. Although by Della Casa's time they were divided into many households, the Rucellai continued to enjoy great power and prestige, as exemplified by the great palace designed for them by Leon Battista Alberti (1404–72).

be polite, pleasant, and well-mannered. If this is not a virtue, it is at least something very similar. And although liberality, courage, or generosity are without doubt far greater and more praiseworthy things than charm and manners, none the less, pleasant habits and decorous manners and words are perhaps no less useful to those who have them than a noble spirit and self-assurance are to others. This is so because everyone must deal with other men and speak to them every day; thus, good manners must also be practised many times daily, whereas justice, fortitude and the other greater and nobler virtues are called into service much more seldom. Generous and magnanimous persons are not called upon to put such virtues into practice on a daily basis; rather, no one could behave in this way very often. Similarly even men who are strong and courageous are rarely required to demonstrate their valour and virtue by their works. Thus, while the latter virtues easily surpass the former in greatness and weightiness, yet the qualities I speak of surpass the others in number and frequency. I could very easily, if it were appropriate, mention to you many men who, though not worthy of high praise in other things, nevertheless are or have been highly esteemed only by reason of their pleasant manner. Thus helped and sustained, they have attained high rank, leaving far behind those who were gifted with those nobler and more outstanding virtues which I mentioned earlier. And, just as pleasant and polite manners have the power to stimulate the benevolence of those with whom we live, rough and uncouth manners lead others to hate and disdain us.

For this reason, even though the laws have not decreed any penalty for unpleasant and rough manners (for this fault has been considered light—and in fact it is not grave), we see none the less that nature herself punishes us severely for it by depriving us of the company and benevolence of others.[3] And just as great sins harm us greatly, these lighter faults are a nuisance and bother us often. Men fear wild beasts

---

[3] Because general laws do not always seem to apply to particular situations, good manners, as most other aspects of social behaviour, depend on individual judgment. Discretion, judgment, and constancy are thus closely linked to social life and betterment. Della Casa is undoubtedly indebted to Aristotle here: "the whole theory of conduct is bound to be an outline only and not an exact system …and matters of conduct and expediency have nothing fixed or invariable about them, any more than have matters of health. And if this is true of the general theory of ethics, still less is exact precision possible in dealing with particular

but have no fear of smaller animals such as mosquitoes or flies; still, because these insects are constant pests, men complain more often about them than about wild beasts. Similarly, most people hate unpleasant and bothersome people as much as, if not more than, evil ones.

Because of this no one will deny that knowing how to be gracious and pleasant in one's habits and manners is a very useful thing to whoever decides to live in cities and among men, rather than in desert wastes or hermit's cells.[4] Moreover, the other virtues require greater resource, without which they amount to little or nothing, while these, quite on their own, are rich and powerful precisely because they involve nothing but words and gestures.

[2]

So that you may learn this lesson more easily, you must know that it will be to your advantage to temper and adapt your manners not according to your own choices but according to the pleasure of those with whom you are dealing and act accordingly. This you must do with moderation,[5] for when someone delights too much in favouring someone else's wishes in conversation or in behaviour he appears to be more of a buffoon or a jester, or perhaps a flatterer, rather than a well-mannered gentleman. And, on the contrary, someone who does not give a thought to another's pleasure or displeasure is boorish, unmannered, and unattractive.

Therefore, our manners are considered pleasant when we take into consideration other people's pleasures and not our own. And if we try to distinguish between the things which generally please the majority of men and those which displease them we can easily discover what

cases of conduct...but the agents themselves have to consider what is suited to the circumstances on each occasion." Aristotle, *The Nicomachean Ethics*, rev. ed., trans. H. Rackham, Loeb Classical Library (Cambridge: Harvard UP, 1934), ii.ii.3–4.

[4]For the question of the *vita civile* and *vita contemplativa*, see the Introduction, pp. 17–18.

[5]The ideal of the golden mean was a classical commonplace. It is found not only in Aristotle (*Nicomachean Ethics*, ii.viii.4–8), and Plato (*Protagoras* 343b), but also in popular Latin authors, such as Horace (*Odes* ii.x.5). Della Casa raises this element to a general guide for social behaviour.

manners are to be shunned and what manners are to be selected for living in society.

Let us say, then, that every act which is disgusting to the senses, unappealing to human desire, and also every act that brings to mind unpleasant matters or whatever the intellect finds disgusting, is unpleasant and ought to be avoided.

[3]

Dirty, foul, repulsive or disgusting things are not to be done in the presence of others, nor should they even be mentioned. And not only is it unpleasant to do them or recall them, but it is also very bothersome to others even to bring them to mind with any kind of behaviour.

Therefore, it is an indecent habit practised by some people who, in full view of others, place their hands on whatever part of their body it pleases them. Similarly, it is not proper for a well-mannered gentleman to prepare to relieve his physical needs in the presence of others. Or, having taken care of his needs, to rearrange his clothing in their presence. And, in my opinion, when returning from nature's summons, he should not even wash his hands in front of decent company, because the reason for his washing implies something disgusting to their imaginations.

For the same reason it is not a proper habit when, as sometimes happens, one sees something disgusting on the road to turn to one's companions and point it out to them. Even less so should one offer something unpleasant to smell, as some insist on doing, placing it even under a companion's nose saying: "Now Sir, please smell how this stinks", when instead he should be saying: "Don't smell this because it stinks."

And just as these and similar actions disturb those senses which they affect, so grinding one's teeth, or whistling, or shrieking, or rubbing together rough stones, or scraping metal is unpleasant to the ear, and a man ought to abstain as much as possible from doing such things. Not only this, but he must avoid singing, especially solo, if his voice is out of tune and unharmonious. But few refrain from doing this; in fact it seems that whoever has the least natural talent for singing is the one who sings most often.

There are also some who cough or sneeze so loudly that they deafen everybody. And some who are so indiscreet in such actions that they spray those near them in the face.

You will also find the type who, when he yawns, howls and brays like an ass; or someone who opens his mouth wide as he begins to speak or carries on with his argument, producing thus a voice, or rather a noise, that a mute makes when he attempts to speak. And these vulgar manners are to be avoided because they are bothersome to the ear and to the eye.

Indeed, a well-mannered man ought to abstain from yawning too much because, besides the above-mentioned reasons, it seems that yawning is caused by boredom and regret, because whoever yawns would much rather be somewhere else and dislikes the company he is with, their conversation, and their activities. Certainly, even though a man is inclined to yawn at any time, it will not occur to him to do it if he is involved in some pleasure or thought; but when he is inactive and indolent he easily remembers to yawn. And so when someone else yawns in the presence of idle and carefree persons, everybody else will immediately start to yawn, as you may have seen many times, as if that person had reminded them of something which they would already have done themselves, had they thought of it first. And many times have I heard learned men say that in Latin the word for yawning is the same as that for lazy and careless.[6] It is therefore advisable to avoid this habit which, as I have said, is unpleasant to the ear, the eyes, and the appetite, because by indulging in it we show that we are not pleased with our companions, and we also give a bad impression of ourselves, that is to say, that we have a drowsy and sleepy spirit which makes us little liked by those with whom we are dealing.

And when you have blown your nose you should not open your handkerchief and look inside, as if pearls or rubies might have descended from your brain.[7] This is a disgusting habit which is not

---

[6]In Latin "oscitare" means "to yawn" and "oscitans" "neglected, careless, negligent, untidy, heedless, thoughtless"; figuratively, "oscitare" means "to be lazy, idle, inactive." See, for example, Cicero, *De oratore* II.xxxiii.144.

[7]In the Renaissance it was believed that mucus descended from the brain. In his work on the human body (*De humani corporis fabrica*), and in his subsequent *Epitome* to it (1543), the Flemish anatomist and surgeon teaching at Padua, Andreas Vesalius (1514–64), writes that the phlegm of the brain descends through an appropriate channel, is distilled by a quadrate gland and then flows out to the palate and the nostrils. *The Epitome of Andreas Vesalius*, trans. R.L. Lind (New York: Macmillan, 1949), 68.

apt to make anyone love you, but rather, if someone loved you already, he is likely to stop there and then. The spirit in the Labyrinth, whoever he may have been, proves this: in order to cool the ardour of Messer Giovanni Boccaccio for a lady he did not know very well, he tells Boccaccio how she squats over ashes and coughs and spits up huge globs.[8]

It is also an unsuitable habit to put one's nose over someone else's glass of wine or food to smell it. By the same token I would not want someone to smell even his own drink or food for fear that some things that men find disgusting may drop from his nose, even if it should not happen. And I would advise you not to offer your glass of wine to someone else after you have had your lips to it and tasted it, unless he were someone very close to you. And even less should you offer a pear or some other fruit into which you have bitten. Do not consider the above things to be of little importance, for even light blows can kill, if they are many.

[4]

I want you to know that in Verona there was once a wise bishop, very learned as a writer, named Messer Giovanni Matteo Giberti.[9] Aside from his other praiseworthy habits, he was also courteous and generous with the noble gentlemen who came and went about him, honouring them in his house with a magnificence which was not overdone, but moderate, as was fitting to a cleric. And it happened that a nobleman by the name of Count Ricciardo was passing by at that time and

---

[8] In the *Corbaccio* of Giovanni Boccaccio (1313–75) the spirit of a deceased man gives vent to a long, fiery series of accusations against his wife and all womankind, touching on subjects from a woman's physiology to the question whether women can claim honour from the fact that the Saviour was born of a woman. See *The Corbaccio*, trans. and ed. Anthony K. Cassell (Urbana: U of Illinois P, 1975), 24–35.

[9] Born at Palermo, where he began his studies, Giovanni Matteo Giberti (1495–1543) was the scion of a Genoese family; he then continued his studies at Rome and Verona. Diplomat, counsellor of Pope Clement VII, bishop of Verona (1524), prelate of great theological erudition and authority, Giberti established a printing press in Verona to publish reliable editions of the Church Fathers. Giberti was deeply involved with the preparations for the Council of Trent, and was an active supporter of reform within the church.

stayed several days with the bishop and his household,[10] which was composed, for the most part, of well-mannered and learned men. Because he seemed to them a very polite gentleman adorned with pleasant manners, they praised and esteemed him highly, except for one small fault in his deportment. The bishop, who was a discerning man, noticed it and, having sought the advice of some of his closer friends, decided that the count ought to be made aware of it without, however, causing him any distress. Since the count was to depart the following morning and had already taken his leave, the bishop called a discreet gentleman of his household and told him to ride out and accompany the count part of the way and then, when he thought the time was right, to tell him politely what they had decided upon together. This gentleman was a man of advanced age, very learned as well as extremely pleasant, a good conversationalist and handsome, all beyond belief, who in his time had much frequented the courts of great lords. He was, and perhaps still is, called Messer Galateo,[11] and it was at his bidding and on his advice that I first started to dictate this treatise.[12] Riding with the count, he soon engaged him in pleasant conversation, moving from one topic to the next, until he thought it was time to return to Verona. Asking for permission to take his leave of the count, with a cheerful countenance, he said delicately: "My

---

[10]In the Renaissance a person's household, his *famiglia* (Latin *familia*) included not only those who were employed by him, but also visitors and friends who would reside with him for a period of time.

[11]Born at Sessa in 1478, Monsignor Galeazzo Florimonte died there as its bishop in 1567. Della Casa describes him in his letter to Cardinal Contarini (*Opere* [Venezia: Casinelli, 1752] III, 43): "Galeazzo Florimonte, who is now bishop of Sessa, is a man adorned not only with every genteel manner, but above all with a chaste and irreproachable manner of living, and he is also very fervent in his religious practices and piety. He is more shrewd and open than anyone else in noticing and reproving his friends' faults, and sometimes he is even a critic who is not quite restrained." He served as pontifical Latin secretary and was an important participant at the Council of Trent. He was a translator of Plato, the author of dialogues on Aristotle and, most significantly for *Galateo*, he began but did not finish his own book of manners, *Il libro delle inezie o un Trattato delle buone creanze*.

[12]Della Casa, as a busy and important diplomat and churchman, did not sit and write his *Galateo* himself, but dictated his text to a secretary who transcribed it for him.

---

lord, my lord bishop extends your lordship his infinite thanks for the honour you have bestowed upon him by entering and dwelling in his humble house. Furthermore, as recompense for all the courtesy you have shown towards him he has commanded me to present you with a gift on his behalf. And he begs you dearly to receive it with a happy heart. This is the gift. You are the most graceful and well-mannered gentleman the bishop thinks he has ever met. For this reason, having carefully observed your manners and having examined them in detail, he has found none which was not extremely pleasant and commendable except for an unseemly motion you make with your lips and mouth at the dinner table, when your chewing makes a strange sound which is very unpleasant to hear. The bishop sends you this message, begging you to try to refrain from doing it, and to accept as a precious gift his loving reprimand and remark, for he is certain no-one else in the world would give you such a gift." The count, who had never before been aware of his fault, blushed slightly on being chastised for it; but, being a worthy man, he quickly recovered himself and said: "Please tell the bishop that men would be far richer than they are if all the gifts they gave each other were like his. And thank him profusely for all the courtesy and generosity he has shown towards me, assuring him that from now on I will diligently and carefully avoid this fault. Now go, and God be with you."

[5]

Now what do we think the bishop and his noble friends would have said to those we sometimes see who, totally oblivious like pigs with their snouts in the swill, never raise their faces nor their eyes, let alone their hands, from the food in front of them? Or to those who eat or rather gulp down their food with both their cheeks puffed out as if they were blowing a trumpet or blowing on a fire? Or to those who soil their hands nearly up to the elbows,[13] and dirty their napkins

---

[13] Although occasional use of the fork is documented from classical times through to the Middle Ages (Ovid mentions it in the *Ars amandi* iii.775 and St. Peter Damian, in the *Institutio monichalis* cap. 40, reproaches the Duchess Teodora Selva for using one), by the sixteenth century the fork had not yet entered into general use either in Italy or elsewhere in Europe. Those who did use it were

worse than their toilet towels? Often they are not ashamed to use these same napkins to wipe away the sweat which, because of their hurry and their over-eating, drips and drops from their foreheads, their faces and from around their necks. They even use them to blow their noses whenever they feel like it. Truly, men like these are not worthy of being received, not just in the very elegant house of that noble bishop, but should even be banished from any place where there are well-mannered men. A well-mannered man must therefore take heed not to smear his fingers so much that his napkin is left soiled, for it is a disgusting thing to see. And even wiping one's fingers on the bread one is about to eat does not seem to be a polite habit.

The servants who wait on gentlemen's tables must not, under any circumstances, scratch their heads—or anything else—in front of their master when he is eating, nor place their hands on any part of the body which is kept covered, nor even appear to do so, as do some careless servants who hold them inside their shirt or keep them behind their backs hidden under their clothes. They must rather keep their hands in sight and out of suspicion, and keep them carefully washed and clean, with no sign of dirt anywhere upon them. Those who serve the dishes of food and the drinks must diligently abstain during that entire time from spitting, coughing and, even more, from sneezing. Since in such actions suspicion of misconduct is just as disturbing to the diners as the certainty of it, so the servants must take care not to give their masters reason to suspect their actions, for in this case what may have taken place disturbs as much as what has taken place.

If you have placed a pear to cook by the fireplace, or roasted bread on the coals, you must not blow on it if it is covered with a few ashes, for the saying is that "there never was wind without rain."[14] You must rather tap the dish gently, or by some other means brush off the ashes. You will not offer your handkerchief to anyone, even though it is fresh out of the laundry, because the man to whom you offer it may not know this and could then be disgusted by it.

---

sometimes derided for doing so. The utensil came into general use in Italy only in the seventeenth century.

[14]The expression is proverbial, and may be compared to the English "where there's smoke there's fire." Della Casa is using the idiom ironically to suggest that one should not blow on a fire on which food is being cooked because of the risk of spraying some saliva on the food.

When one speaks with someone, he should not get so close to the man that he breathes on his face, for you will find that many men do not like to smell someone else's breath, even though it may not have any bad odour to it. These and other such manners are unpleasant and should be avoided for, as I said above, they could bother some of the senses of those with whom we are dealing.

Let us now mention those manners which are not obnoxious to any of the senses in particular, but still offend the majority of persons when they are committed.

[6]

You must know that men naturally desire different and varied things: some want to satisfy their wrath, some their gluttony, others their sexual desires, others their avarice, and still others some other appetite. When dealing with other men, however, it does not seem that one asks, or could ask or desire, any of the above-mentioned things, in as much as these appetites are not evident in their manners of behaviour or in their speech, but elsewhere. They therefore desire whatever can facilitate this act of social intercourse; and this appears to be kindness, honour, and pleasure, or some similar thing. For this reason one must not say or do anything which may give an indication that one holds the other person in little affection or harbours a low opinion of him. Thus, the habit of many people of falling asleep quite eagerly wherever a respectable group of persons is sitting in conversation appears to be impolite. By doing this, they show that they have a low opinion of the company and appreciate very little indeed both the company and the discussion. Not to mention that whoever falls asleep, especially if he is in an uncomfortable position—which is inevitable—most of the time succumbs to the tendency to do something which is unpleasant to see or to hear. Very often he wakes up sweaty and slobbery.

For this same reason it appears to be a bothersome habit to get up where other persons are sitting in conversation and pace about the room. There are some who so fidget, writhe, stretch, and yawn, turning first to one side, then to the other, that it looks as if they have just caught the fever. These are obvious signs that they are unhappy with the company.

Those who occasionally pull a letter out of their pockets and read it act just as badly. Someone who pulls out his nail clippers and devotes himself to his manicure acts even worse, appearing to hold the company in no esteem at all and so tries to find some other amusement for himself in order to pass the time.

One must not indulge in the habits of some other men, such as humming to oneself, or tapping one's fingers, or moving one's leg to and fro, for they indicate that the person does not care for others.

In addition, one must not turn one's back to someone, nor hold one's leg so high that those parts covered up by clothing become visible, for these acts should not be done among persons one respects. However, it is true that if a gentleman did them among very close friends or in the presence of a friend of lower social rank he would show not arrogance but rather love and intimacy.

A man must stand erect and not lean against or over someone else. When he speaks he must not elbow others, as many are in the habit of doing with every sentence, saying: "Isn't that right? What do you say about that? What about Mr So-and-so?" all the while jabbing you with their elbows.

[7]

Everyone must dress well according to his status and age, because if he does otherwise it seems that he disdains other people. For this reason the people of Padua used to take offence when a Venetian gentleman would go about their city in a plain overcoat as if he thought he was in the country.[15] Not only should clothing be of fine material, but a man must also try to adapt himself as much as he can to the sartorial style of other citizens and let custom guide him, even though it may seem to him to be less comfortable and attractive than previous fashions. If everyone in your town wears his hair short, you should not wear it long; and where other citizens wear a beard, you should not be clean shaven,[16] for this is a way of contradicting others, and such con-

---

[15]Padua, with its ancient and famous university (founded in 1222), was conquered by Venice and incorporated into the Venetian state in 1405. The city and its university became an important intellectual centre for the Republic.

[16]Della Casa is referring to the changes in fashion brought about by foreign, especially Spanish, influence in Italy. Beards in particular were significant for Dalla Casa because they had princely associations in Florence.

tradictions, in your dealings with others, should be avoided unless they are necessary, as I will tell you later. This, more than any other bad habit, renders us despicable to most other persons. You should not, therefore, oppose common custom in these practices, but rather moderately adapt yourself to them, so that you will not be the only one in your neighbourhood to wear a long gown down to your feet while everyone else wears a short one, just past the belt. It is like having a very pug face, that is to say, something against the general fashion of nature, so that everybody turns around to look at it. So it is also with those who do not dress according to the prevailing style but according to their own taste, with beautiful long hair, or with a very short-cropped beard or a clean-shaven face, or who wear caps, or great big hats in the German fashion. Everyone turns around to look at them and crowds around to see them, as one does, for example, with those people who seem ready to come to blows with everyone in their neighbourhood. Clothes must also fit well and suit the wearer, for men who wear rich and noble clothes that are so ill-made that they do not seem made for them indicate one of two things: either they have no conception that they could please or displease others, or they have no conception of what grace and measure are. With their manners these men then make their companions suspect that they have a low opinion of them, and so are ill-received by most groups and are not well liked.

[8]

There are others who are more than suspect, for they act and behave in such a manner that it is impossible to put up with them. They always cause delay, annoyance, and discomfort for everybody; they are never ready, never orderly, never satisfied. When everybody is ready to sit down at the table, for example, and the food is ready to be served, and everyone has washed his hands, they ask for pen and paper, or for a urinal, or complain that they missed their daily exercise and say: "It's still early. Surely you can wait a while. What's the hurry this morning?" and by being concerned so much with themselves and their own needs, totally oblivious of others, they hold up the entire company. Moreover, they want to have an advantage over others in all things; they want to sleep in the best beds, in the most beautiful rooms, and sit in the most comfortable chairs and take the place of honour, and expect to be served or seated before anyone else, and never like anything unless they themselves thought it up, turning up their noses at everything else, and think that others ought to wait for them before taking a meal, going out riding, playing a game, or being entertained.

Some other people are so touchy, contrary-minded, or strange that nothing can be done to please them. They always answer with a sour face, no matter what is said to them. They never cease yelling at or scolding their servants, and keep the entire company in constant misery. "Some fine hour you called me this morning! Look here how well you shined this shoe! And you didn't come to church with me! You ass, I don't know what's keeping me from punching you right in the snout!" All of these are unsuitable and rude manners which must be avoided like the plague. Even if a man were full of humility and had displayed such manners not out of malice but out of carelessness and bad habits, he would still be hated because his outward behaviour would suggest he was haughty. For arrogance is nothing else but lack of respect for others, and, as I said at the beginning, everybody wishes to be respected even if he does not deserve it.

Not long ago there was in Rome a worthy man gifted with a sharp mind and profound learning and his name was Messer Ubaldino Bandinelli.[17] This man used to say that whenever he came or went from the Vatican palace, although the streets were full of noble courtiers, prelates, and lords, and also of poor, or middle-class, or even low-class people, none the less he never thought he met anyone who was more or less worthy than he was. Undoubtedly there were few he could see that matched him, if we keep in mind his own virtue which truly was very great. However, in these matters men must not be judged in this way; rather, they must be weighed with the miller's scales, not those of the goldsmith.[18] It is proper to accept them readily not for what they are truly worth but rather, as with money, for their stated value. Therefore, nothing must be done in front of those people

---

[17]Ubaldino Bandinelli (1494–1551) was the learned Florentine bishop of Montefiascone and Corneto. When Della Casa returned to Florence in 1524, Bandinelli, who was still a subdeacon in Florence, became his poetry teacher. On his untimely death Della Casa grieved, writing "This man led me through the steep windings of the Castalian path, this man taught me the lyric art" in the Latin ode "De Ubaldino Bandinelli" in *Opere* I, 33 and 285.

[18]That is, with large rather than with small scales.

we wish to please which denotes lordship rather than companionship. Every action of ours, instead, must imply reverence and respect towards the people in whose company we find ourselves.

For this reason, whatever is not worthy of blame at the proper time may be reprehensible in another context, or with other persons, such as speaking roughly to servants, or reprimanding them—as we mentioned above—or, worse still, beating them. Doing such things is a way of lording it over someone and exercising one's jurisdiction, which no one does in front of those one respects without shocking the company and ruining the conversation, especially if it is done at the dinner table, which should be a place for merriment and not indignation. Thus, Messer Currado Gianfigliazzi acted correctly when he did not prolong the discussion with his cook Chichibio so as not to trouble his guests, even though the servant deserved great punishment for having chosen to please his girl Brunetta rather than his lord.[19] If Currado had made even less of a fuss, he would have been even more praiseworthy, for it was not right to threaten his servant and call upon the name of the Lord blasphemously, as he did.

Returning to our matter, however, I will say that it is not pleasant that someone should lose his temper at the table, no matter what happens. If he should become upset he should not show it nor give any indication of his anger, for the reason I have already mentioned, especially if you have strangers dining with you; you have called them to enjoy themselves and now you are causing them anxiety. When we see other people eat bitter, tart fruits our own mouths will pucker; similarly when we see someone else become upset, this will upset us as well.

[9]

Those people who want what is opposite to the wishes of most people are called contrary-minded, as the word itself shows; for contrary is a

---

[19]In order to please the servant-girl Brunetta, the cook Chichibio let her eat a leg from the crane he was roasting for a feast his master Currado Gianfigliazzi was giving. When, at the feast, Currado questioned the cook about the missing leg, Chichibio answered saying that cranes have only one leg. Not to be outdone, Currado led Chichibio and the guests to the pond where he kept cranes. At that time, all the birds were resting, standing on one leg and keeping the other tucked away under their wing. Currado clapped his hands, woke the birds, and

synonym for opposite. You can therefore easily judge on your own how useful being contrary is to those who want to have the affection and the love of other people, for it consists in being opposed to the pleasure of others and this tends to make enemies rather than friends. Those who wish to have the affection of others should always try to avoid this vice, for it produces neither pleasure nor goodwill, but rather hatred and displeasure. On the contrary, if there is no danger of harm or shame, one should make other people's desires one's own, and do and say rather what others like to hear than what you yourself like.

One should not be either uncouth or awkward, but pleasant and friendly, for there is no difference between the myrtle and the butcher's-broom except that one is a cultivated plant and the other a wild one.[20]

I want you to know that a man is considered pleasant if his manners conform to the common practices between friends, whereas someone who is eccentric will, in all situations, appear to be a stranger, that is, alien. On the contrary, men who are affable and polite will appear to have friends and acquaintances wherever they may be.

For this reason it is advisable to accustom oneself to greet, speak, and answer gracefully, and to treat everyone like a neighbour or a friend. Those who are never kind to anybody behave wrongly when they eagerly say no to everything, or appreciate no honour or kindness which is rendered to them. They are like foreigners and barbarians. They do not appreciate visitors, nor do they like company; they do not enjoy witty remarks or pleasantries, and refuse all offers. If someone should say: "A short time back Messer So-and-so asked me to extend his greetings." They answer: "And what am I to do with his greetings?" Or if someone says: "Messer So-and-so asked how you were." They respond: "Let him come and take my pulse." These persons really deserve not to be well liked by others.

It is not fitting to be melancholy or distracted in the company of others. This may be accepted of people who have long pursued studies in the arts which, as I have heard, are called "liberal arts," but it

---

as they lowered their other leg began to chastize Chichibio. But the servant quickly pointed out that if Currado had done the same for the roasted crane that bird too would have brought out the missing leg. At this point Currado accepted the *bon mot* and overlooked his cook's misdemeanour. *Decameron* VI, 4.

[20]Myrtle and butcher's-broom are very similar, but the second has thorns and the first does not; butcher's-broom (pungitopo) is closely related to holly.

should not, under any condition, be allowed of other people.[21] Even those who are allowed such introspection would do well to withdraw from the company of others when they want to devote themselves to thinking.

[10]

It is also not appropriate, especially for men, to be overly sensitive and fastidious, for to deal in this way with other people is called not companionship but servitude. There certainly are some who are so sensitive and easily hurt that to live or to be with them is nothing more than finding oneself surrounded by many fine glass objects, for they fear every little blow, and so they must be treated and respected like fine crystal. If you are not quick or solicitous enough in greeting them, visiting them, answering them, or paying your respects to them, they become as distressed with you as another man would if you had mortally insulted him. If you do not grant them all of their titles correctly, bitter quarrels and deathly hatreds immediately ensue. "You called me Sir and not Lord. And why don't you call me Your Lordship? I, after all, do call you signor Such-and-such." Or, "I did not have my proper place at the table. And yesterday you did not deign to come visit me at home, as I had come to visit you the day before yesterday. These are not ways of dealing with someone such of my rank."

These people truly bring others to the point of not being able to suffer their presence, for they indulge immoderately in self-love, and being so pre-occupied with themselves they have little time available to love anyone else. Besides, as I said at the beginning, men expect from the company of others those pleasures which they themselves seek. To be with such fussy people whose friendship tears as easily as a thin veil is not, therefore, a benefit but a burden. For this reason such company is not pleasant, but is highly unpleasant. Such sensitivity and such fastidiousness are best left to women.

[11]

In conversation, one can err in many various ways. First, the choice of topic should not be either frivolous or sordid, since listeners will not

---

[21]Melancholia was often seen as a scholar's affliction.

pay attention to such subjects nor take pleasure in them. On the contrary, they will despise both the discussions and the speaker. Also, one must not discuss subtle or arcane topics, for the majority of people can hardly understand them. Instead, one must diligently choose a topic so that no one in the group will be embarrassed or ashamed. Nor should anyone speak of filthy matters even if they were pleasant to hear, for honourable people should try to please others with honourable subjects.

Neither in jest nor in earnest should anyone say anything against God or his saints, no matter how witty and pleasant it may be. This sin was often committed by the group of noble youths in the *Decameron* of our Messer Giovanni Boccaccio, and for this they should be chastised harshly by all discerning people.[22] Remember that to speak lightly of God is not only the sign of a wicked and sinful man, but also the vice of a man with no manners. It is unpleasant to hear, and you will find many who will flee from a place where God's name is spoken of profanely. Not only should one speak reverently of God, but in every discussion one should be careful that one's words do not bear witness against one's life and deeds, for men detest to see in others even the vices which they themselves have.

Similarly, it is not proper to speak of things which are critical of present times and people, even if these things, in their own time and place, would be both good and respectable. Let Friar Nastagio's sermons then not be mentioned to young women intent on amusing themselves, as that fine fellow who lived near San Brancazio, not far from you, used to do.[23]

---

[22] In the middle of the sixteenth century the religious climate in Italy began to engender a more conservative, respectful, and careful attitude towards ecclesiastical subjects. Consequently, the satirical and unflattering portrayal of clergy in the fourteenth century and the spirit underlying much of Boccaccio's *Decameron* became suspect. In order to save what was already considered the masterpiece of Italian narrative prose from being placed on the Index and thus banned to the general readership, the offensive passages and references were either altered or eliminated, thus giving birth to a long series of expurgated editions of Boccaccio's saucy tales.

[23] Puccio di Ranieri is a character in *Decameron* III, 4. When his young wife made amorous advances to him, the saintly and much older Puccio restrained her urges by telling her about the life of Christ or of Mary Magdalene, or by recounting to her the sermons of a local saintly friar, Nastagio. Puccio lived in the Florentine parish of San Pancrazio, which is where the Rucellai also had their

At a feast or at the table one should not tell sad stories, nor mention nor remind people of wounds, diseases, deaths, and plagues, or any other painful subject. And if anyone else lapses into this sort of conversation, one must gently and correctly change the subject and provide a happier and more suitable one. Even so, I have heard one of my distinguished neighbours say that men have a great need to cry as well as to laugh. He claimed that for this reason those sad stories we call tragedies were at first devised, so that when performed in theatres—as they were in those times—they would bring tears to the eyes of whoever needed it so that they would be relieved by crying.[24] What-ever the case, it is not fitting to sadden those with whom one is talking, especially where people are gathered for festivities and pleasure rather than for mourning. If there should be someone who is so ill that he needs a good cry, the cure is very simple: either give him strong mustard to eat, or put him in a room full of smoke.[25] For this reason there is no excuse for Filostrato who proposed that the company, which was interested only in pleasant things, should instead hear stories full of sorrow and death.[26] It is better, then, to avoid talking about sad matters and, if necessary, to remain silent instead.

Those who are constantly talking about their children, their wives or their nursemaids, are equally at fault. "Yesterday my boy made me laugh so much. Listen to this...You have never seen a more lovable son than my Momo...My wife is such that...My Cecchina says that...I am

---

homes. Della Casa's nephew, being a Rucellai, would have dwelt in that parish as well. In Boccaccio's novel, Puccio was actually an old man married to a much younger woman. The narrator's description of him as "that young man" is merely part of the persona Della Casa is creating.

[24]The reference is to Aristotle and to his concept of catharsis, especially as it applies to tragedy. "Through pity and fear it [tragedy] effects relief to these and similar emotions." Aristotle, *The Poetics*, trans. W. Hamilton Fyfe, Loeb Classical Library (Cambridge: Harvard UP, 1973), vi.2, p. 23. The meaning of "relief" (catharsis) was still being debated in the sixteenth century; see for example Piccolomini's commentary on Aristotle's *Poetics* (1575 ed.), p. 100.

[25]The narrator seems to be mocking the entire concept of catharsis by suggesting that tears brought about by smoke or strong spices can also alleviate the soul and restore a person's psychological well-being. Rather than Della Casa's opinion, this is more an element of the characterization of the uneducated elderly narrator.

[26]Filostrato, one of the youths who narrate the stories in the *Decameron*, sets the topic of unhappy loves for the fourth day.

sure you would not believe how bright she is ..."[27] No-one has so little to do that he has the time to answer or even to listen to such nonsense, and so it irritates everyone.

[12]

Those who describe their dreams in great detail and with great enthusiasm making such fuss that one is left exhausted just hearing them, behave wrongly, especially since, in most cases, it would be a waste of time to listen to the greatest achievement of this type of person, even if they had accomplished it while awake. Thus, one should not bore others with such worthless things as dreams, especially since most dreams are generally silly. Although I very often hear that the ancient sages included a great many dreams in their books, written with deep knowledge and in fine style, it is not suitable for us unlearned men and for the common folk to do this in our conversation.[28] Indeed, of all the dreams I have been told—but I pay attention to few of these— I have never heard any that was worth the noise. That is, except for one, experienced once by Messer Flaminio Tomarozzo, a Roman gentleman, not at all unlearned or thickheaded, but enlightened and sharp witted.[29] In his sleep, he thought he was sitting in the house of his neighbour, a very rich apothecary, and then, for one reason or

---

[27] Momo is the affectionate diminutive for Girolamo, Cecchina for Francesca.

[28] Dreams and their meaning appear often in classical sources and thus rekindled Renaissance humanist interest in them. See Xenophon, *Cyropaedia* VIII.4, p. 21; Plato, *Republic* IX.1; Aristotle, *On the interpretation of dreams* chapter 2; as well as Lucian and Cicero. The ancients categorized dreams (see for example, Virgil, *Aeneid* VI.890) and dreams played a significant role in classical literature, as Della Casa has noted. During the Middle Ages, the distinction was primarily between those dreams that derived from the animal nature of man (the sensitive soul) which were dismissed as false and simply visions of an altered reality, and those dreams that arose from the mind (the intellectual soul) which could be informed by Divine Revelation. This essentially Platonic doctrine was widely held in the Renaissance.

[29] Little is known of Flaminio Tomarozzo, a correspondent of Della Casa's friend Pietro Bembo, the celebrated Venetian author, arbiter of taste and later cardinal. Della Casa mentions him in passing in his biography of Gaspare Contarini (*Opere* III, p. 73).

another, the mob went on a rampage and began to loot the shop. One took an electuary, another a confection,[30] one man took one thing, another man something else and swallowed it right there and then so that, in less than an hour, there was not a phial, a jar, a pot, or a box that was not empty and dry. A small flask remained, full of a very clear liquid, which many smelled but none would taste. In a short time he saw an old man of great stature and with a venerable appearance come in and look at the poor apothecary's empty boxes and jars, spilled and scattered about, and almost all of them broken. Catching sight of the small flask I mentioned, he picked it up and drank all the liquid it contained to the last drop. Having done this, he left as everyone else had done. Messer Flaminio was much taken aback by this, so, turning to the apothecary, he asked: "Master, who was that man, and why did he drink so heartily the water in the flask that everybody else had refused?" And he thought that the apothecary answered saying: "My son, that was the Lord God. The water which he alone drank and which everybody else, as you saw, despised and refused was good judgement which, as you may have understood, no man is willing to taste by any means."

One can tell and listen to this kind of dream with great pleasure and profit, for it is more like the thoughts of a quick mind or, shall I say, a perception by the senses, than the visions of a sleepy head. But we must forget and dismiss together with our sleep the formless and senseless dreams of our equals, but not those of the learned or of the virtuous, for even in their sleep they are wiser and better than the unlearned and the wicked.

[13]

Although it seems that there is nothing vainer than dreams, there is something which is even emptier: lies. What one experiences in dreams has some grounding in reality or in the emotions, but lies have no basis in either reality or in the imagination. For this reason, one asks that men's minds and ears be bothered even less with lies than with dreams, even though lies are sometimes accepted as the truth. In

---

[30]An electuary was a medicinal powder mixed with honey or some other sweet substance; a confection would have been any medicinal compound.

the long run, liars are neither believed nor listened to, like those people whose words are meaningless and whose speech is more or less empty air.

You will meet many men who lie without intent of malice or personal advantage or with no wish to do damage or bring shame upon anybody, but because they like lying, much as someone who drinks not because he is thirsty but because he likes wine. Others tell lies for their own aggrandisement, boasting, claiming great accomplishments or great knowledge for themselves.

It is also possible to keep silent and lie, and this is done with actions and deeds. You will see some of middle or lower rank do this when they bear themselves with great solemnity and behave pompously, speaking so rhetorically, or rather pontificating, eager to sit in judgement on anything and strutting about so much that it is a deadly nuisance just to watch them.

You will find some who, although they have no greater wealth than others, have so many gold chains around their necks and rings on their fingers and so many broaches on their hats and here and there on their clothing that it would not befit the Seigneur of Castiglione himself.[31] Their manners are full of affectation and self-importance arising first from arrogance and ultimately from vanity, and these must be avoided because they are unpleasant and unbefitting. Know that in many of the best cities it is forbidden by law that a wealthy man parade about attired much more gorgeously than a poor man,[32] for it would seem that the poor are wronged when others, even in

---

[31] In order to impress the girl Nuccia, Guccio Imbratta in *Decameron* VI, 10, gives himself the airs of a very rich foreigner by claiming to be the "Siri di Ciastiglione," that is, the rich and powerful Seigneur de Châtillon-sur-Marne. The similarity of title with Count Baldassare Castiglione, author of the *Courtier*, causes our uneducated narrator to confuse the original Châtillon, italianized by Boccaccio as Ciastiglione, with the contemporary writer and the town of Castiglione.

[32] Almost every state in Europe, including Della Casa's native Florence, enacted sumptuary legislation to enforce distinctions between classes in society and to discourage wasteful, conspicuous consumption. The very fact that such laws were regularly re-enacted indicates that they were largely ignored, as Della Casa implies. These sumptuary laws grew in importance in Italy with the introduction of new fashions from Northern Europe. The spread of luxury objects of apparel, especially the new masculine styles of gold hat brooches, earrings, and chains diverted much capital from useful production into personal consumption, helping

matters of appearance, show themselves to be superior to them. So one must diligently take care not to fall into these silly habits.

Nor should a man boast of his nobility, his titles, his riches, least of all his intelligence. Nor should he praise at length, as some do, his past deeds and accomplishments, nor those of his ancestors, for in so doing it seems that he wants either to challenge those present who show themselves to be or who aspire to be equally as noble, as well off, and as capable, or to overwhelm them if they are of lesser stature, even appearing to chastise them for their humble origins and their poverty. In both cases such behaviour displeases everybody. Thus, one should neither humble nor unduly exalt oneself. Instead, one should rather subtract something from one's merits than add something to them with words, for even good qualities, if exaggerated, are displeasing. You should know that those who humble themselves beyond measure in their speech and refuse all honours that are their obvious due show far greater arrogance in this than those who usurp these honours without real merit. For this reason one could perhaps say that Giotto did not deserve the praises some people have showered upon him for refusing to be called "master," seeing that he was not just a master, but without a doubt a great master in his day.[33] Leaving aside whether Giotto deserves praise or blame, it is clear that a man who despises what other men desire shows that he reproaches or despises other men. To despise glory and honour, which other men value so highly, is to glorify and exalt oneself above all other men because no man in his right mind will refuse precious things unless he feels already abundantly provided with others he values even more highly. For this reason we should neither boast of our blessings nor despise them, for to boast of them is to chastise others for their failings, and to despise them is to deride their virtues. As far as possible, one should keep quiet about oneself, and if the situation forces us to speak of ourselves, then it is a pleasant habit to speak truthfully and modestly, as I have already said.

Therefore, those who delight in pleasing others must avoid as much as they can that common habit of many who express their opinion on

---

to ruin patrician families and widening even more the gap between classes. In former republics like Florence these changes would have been even more marked.

[33]Della Casa is alluding to Boccaccio's novella about the painter Giotto (1267–1337) and Messer Forese da Rabatta, a politician and a jurist (*Decameron* VI, 5).

any subject with so much shyness that it is a slow death to listen to them, especially if they are considered to be intelligent, knowledgeable men. "Sir, I beg your lordship's pardon if I cannot suitably express myself. I will speak in rough terms, like the simple man I am, according to the little I know. I am certain your lordship will mock me afterwards, still, in order to obey your wish ..." they work the question so much, and go to such lengths without ever resolving it, that even the most subtle problem could have been unravelled with far fewer words in a much shorter space of time.

Equally tedious and deceiving are those men who, in the manner of their speech and their actions, show themselves lowly and unworthy. Although it is obvious that they are entitled to precedence and to the place of honour, they will place themselves at the back. It is then an unparalleled task to get them to move forward, for they keep moving back like a mule shying away from something. When approaching a doorway, one always has a difficult time with people such as these because, for no reason in the world will they want to go through first. They will step aside or retrace their steps, and then shield and protect themselves with hands and arms, so that every few steps one must engage in battle with them thus disrupting the pleasant conversation or the business at hand.

[14]

As you can see, we have named ceremonies with a foreign word,[34] as is done for things for which our own language does not have a name; for it is evident that our ancestors did not know these ceremonies and so could not give them a name. In my judgement, ceremonies are, because of their emptiness, very little removed from lies and dreams. Consequently, we can very easily treat them together and join them in our treatise, seeing that the occasion to speak of them has arisen.

According to what a good man has explained to me several times, those solemnities which the clergy uses towards God and sacred things during divine services at the altar are rightly called ceremonies. But when men first began to pay respect to each other in artificial, inap-

---

[34] It was believed—incorrectly—that the Latin word *caeremonia* derived from the name of the earth goddess Ceres.

propriate ways, and to call each other Lord and Sir, bowing and bending and writhing as a sign of respect, and uncovering their heads, and
giving themselves exquisite titles, and kissing each others' hands as if
they were sacred like a priest's, someone who did not have a name for
this new, silly habit called it a ceremony. I think it was done in mockery, just as drinking and carousing are often called in jest a "triumph."
This habit is certainly not native to us but is foreign and barbarous,
only recently brought into Italy from where I do not know. Our poor
country, brought low and humiliated in fact and effect, grows and is
honoured only in vain words and superficial titles.[35]

If we consider the intention of those who use them, ceremonies are
an empty show of honour and reverence towards the person to whom
they are directed, consisting of appearances, words, titles, and saluta-
tions. I say vain because we appear to honour those whom we hold in
no special reverence and those whom we sometimes hold in contempt. None the less, in order not to stray from the habit of others,
we refer to them as "the most illustrious Sir So-and-so," and "the most
excellent Lord Such-and-such." Similarly, we sometimes present ourselves to someone to whom we would rather do a disservice than a service as "your most devoted servant."

Ceremonies should then be seen not simply as lies, as I have said,
but also as infamies and treacheries. But because the words and titles I
have mentioned have lost their strength and have been worn down
like iron by the constant use we make of them, one should not listen
to them as seriously as one does to other words, nor interpret them
literally. The truth of this is evident when in our daily experience we
meet someone we have never seen before and for some reason we need
to speak to him without knowing his actual rank. More often than
not we would rather say too much than too little. Thus, we will call
him "Sir" or "Gentleman" even if he is only a cobbler or a barber
dressed decently enough. In the past titles used to be determined and
distinguished by papal or imperial privilege,[36] and these titles could
not be withheld without insulting and injuring the bearer, nor, on the

---

[35]The Spanish domination of the Italian peninsula after 1529 had a profound
effect upon Italian manners, styles of dress, etiquette, and even the Italian language. Della Casa was particularly hostile to the Spaniards and their influence.
Castiglione reflects the same underlying hostility in his *Courtier*.

[36]Italy, lacking a central government, recognized those titles of honour granted

contrary, could they be granted without mockery to those who did not possess them. Similarly, nowadays, one must grant much more liberally these titles and other similar indications of honour because custom—far too powerful a lord—has greatly privileged the men of our times with them. This habit, then, so beautiful and becoming on the outside, is inside totally empty, and consists in appearances without substance and in words without meaning. This does not allow us, however, to change it. On the contrary, we are obliged to abide by it because it is a fault of the times, not of ourselves. Ceremony, however, must be carried out with moderation.

[15]

For this reason one should keep in mind that ceremonies are observed for three reasons: for profit, for vanity, or out of duty. Every lie told for one's own profit is a fraud, a sin, and a dishonest thing, for one never lies honestly. This is the sin committed by flatterers. These men appear to be our friends and pander to our wishes, whatever they may be, not for our good but for their own profit, not to please us but to deceive us. And, although this vice may appear to be a pleasant habit, none the less it is not fitting for a well-mannered man because it is in itself despicable and harmful, for it is not acceptable that one should give pleasure by causing harm. Because ceremonies are, as we have said, lies and false flatteries, whenever we use them for our own profit we behave as disloyal and evil men. Therefore, no ceremony is to be used for this purpose.

[16]

Now there remains for me to speak of those ceremonies which are observed out of duty and those which are observed out of vanity. It is

---

through the authority of the papacy or the Holy Roman Empire, the two powers that fought for dominion over the peninsula during the early Middle Ags. Often papal (Guelf) cities were ruled by papal vicars and imperial (Ghibelline) cities by imperial vicars. Although these local rulers eventually developed into de facto princes, they initially claimed their authority from pope or emperor.

in no way fitting to forego the former, because the man who does not observe them not only displeases but also offends. It has happened many times that swords have been drawn merely because one citizen, meeting another on the street, did not show him due honour. For, as I have said, the strength of custom is very great and in such matters should be considered a law. For this reason the man who addresses another man saying "You" is not paying him a gratuitous compliment, unless the other is from a very low class. On the contrary, if he addressed him as "Thou" he would be detracting something from him, showing him disrespect and doing him harm by using that word which is customarily used only for the common people and the peasantry.[37]

Although other nations and other times had other customs in this regard, none the less we have our own, and there is no point in discussing which of two customs is better. So it is advisable for us to obey not what is the best but what is the modern custom, just as we obey even those laws which are less than good until the state or whoever has the power to do so changes them. Thus, in the land where we dwell we must diligently assume the gestures and the words which usage and modern custom normally employ in welcoming, greeting, and addressing each man in his own station; and when dealing with society we must abide by these practices.

The admiral Rugger de Loria, when speaking with King Peter of Aragon, many times addressed him as "Thou," as in fact the custom of his times happened to dictate.[38] Nevertheless, we address our kings as "Your Majesty" and "Your Highness" both orally and in letters. In fact,

---

[37]Renaissance Italian used the "voi" form for polite address, and the "tu" form for familiar address. This pattern is still in use in Central and Southern Italian dialects. Governmental attempts in the 1920s and 1930s to re-establish the "voi" as the correct form of polite address in standard Italian were not successful, and the "Lei" form, which had entered Italian in the late sixteenth century as a result of foreign influences (especially Spanish), has remained the norm for standard Italian.

[38]*Decameron* v, 6. Ruggero di Lauria (c.1245–1305), admiral of the Aragonese fleet, fought brilliantly against the Angevin rulers of Southern Italy. The king the narrator mentions is probably Peter III of Aragon (1239–85), king of Aragon from 1276 and of Sicily from 1282, and the ruler during the revolt of the Sicilian Vespers. Boccaccio (*Decameron* v, 6), however, refers to "Federigo re di Cicilia," that is, Frederick II of Aragon (reigned 1296–1337). It is the uneducated narrator who makes the mistake.

just as he observed the custom of his times, so we must not disregard the custom of ours.

These I call obligatory formalities, for they do not originate from our own desire or from our own free will, but are imposed upon us by law, that is, by general custom. In matters that do not have anything evil about them but on the contrary seem to have a semblance of courtesy, it is desirable or rather necessary to obey general customs and not to dispute or disagree with them.

Although to kiss as a sign of reverence is strictly suited only for relics of saints' bodies or other sacred things, none the less, if in your neighbourhood it is the custom when leaving to say, "Sir, I kiss your hand," or, "I am your servant," or even, "I am your bounden slave" you must not be more reticent than others. On the contrary, when leaving or writing you must greet and take your leave according to what not reason but custom dictates, and not as one used to do or should have done, but as one does. And you must not say: "What is he a master of, anyway?" or "Has this man become my parish priest, that I should kiss his hand?" For the man who is accustomed to being called "Sir" by others and similarly to call others "Sir" will think that you disdain him or that you are insulting him when you call him by name, or "Mister," or decide to address him as "You."

As I have told you above, these words indicating position or service, and others such as these, from being too much in people's mouths have lost most of their harshness and, like some herbs left in water, have rather turned to pulp and have softened. One should not shun them, as do some rude and boorish persons who would rather have people begin their letters to emperors and kings in this manner: "If you and your children are well, that is fine; I am well too."[39] They claim that this was the salutation used by the ancient Latin men when addressing letters to the Comune in Rome.[40] If one followed this criterion of returning to the past, everyone would revert, little by little, to eating acorns.[41] But there are, in these obligatory ceremonies, certain rules that must be observed so as not to appear to others to be full of vanity or pride.

---

[39] A translation of the Latin greeting: "Si tu vales, bene est; ego quidem valeo."

[40] Again a mistake of the uneducated old man; it should read "Senate" or "Magistrates."

[41] The Renaissance believed in a "Great Chain of Being" linking all creation

First of all, one must consider the country where one lives, for every custom is not acceptable everywhere. Perhaps what is customary for Neapolitans, whose city is rich in men of great lineage and barons with great power, would not do, for example, for the Lucchesi or Florentines who are, for the most part, merchants and simple gentlemen and do not have among them any princes, marquises, or barons.[42] Therefore, the lordly and pompous manners of Naples transferred to Florence would be as oversized and superfluous as the clothes of a large man placed on a midget; and equally the manners of the Florentines would appear meager and inadequate to the noble minds and temperament of the Neapolitans.

And just because the gentlemen of Venice use an inordinate number of compliments amongst themselves on account of the positions they hold and the votes they cast, it would not be fitting for the magistrates of Rovigo, or the citizens of Asolo to maintain, for no reason at all, that same degree of solemnity in greeting each other.[43] However, it seems to me that that entire region has fallen somewhat into this nonsense, perhaps because of idleness, or perhaps because they have acquired them from their masters in Venice (for everyone eagerly follows in the steps of his master, though he knows not the reason why).[44]

---

from the lowest elements on earth to the celestial sphere of God Himself. Italian Renaissance Neoplatonic thinkers wrote that each person largely determined his place on this scale through his own free will. Della Casa is alluding to this concept (most effectively described by Giovanni Pico della Mirandola in his treatise *On the Dignity of Man*), but in a popular form. See also Castiglione's *Courtier*, IV, pp. 341 ff. in the Penguin translation.

[42]Lucca and Florence were Italian republics and hence did not dispense noble titles. Della Casa is subtly comparing these two states, the one (Lucca) which managed to remain a republic and free from foreign domination, the other (Florence) which after 1537 had become a hereditary principality under the Medici supported by Spanish troops.

[43]Venice was (and remained until 1797 when it was overthrown by Napoleon) a republic, hence Della Casa's reference to the importance of the elected office of Venetian patricians and the significance of their votes. Rovigo and Asolo are small towns close to Venice, subject to the Serenissima, and favourite vacation spots for wealthy Venetians. Asolo, in the province of Treviso, is not far from where Della Casa lived when he was writing *Galateo*.

[44]The expansion of Venice to the Italian mainland after 1380 led to the spread of Venetian culture not only because of the influence of the *città dominante* but

Moreover, one must respect the time, age and status both of the man with whom we use these formalities and of ourselves. With busy men we must completely eliminate formalities, or at least cut them as short as possible, and preferably imply them rather than express them. The courtiers in Rome know how to do this very well. In other places, however, formalities are a great obstacle to business and are very boring. "Put your hat back on," says the busy judge who has no time to waste; and the man before him first performs a number of bows, with much shuffling of feet, and then, speaking slowly, answers: "My Lord, I am fine as I am." "Nevertheless," says the judge, "Put your hat back on." And the man, bending two or three times to each side and bowing to the ground answers in a solemn voice: "I beseech your Lordship to allow me to do my duty." And this encounter lasts so long and so much time is wasted that the judge could very nearly have completed his morning's business in the meantime.

Therefore, although it is every person's duty to honour judges and men of higher rank than himself, none the less where time does not allow it this becomes a bothersome activity which must be either avoided or curtailed.

It is not suitable for young men to use those same formalities among themselves that older men use; nor is it fitting for the lower and middle classes to use those that aristocrats affect among themselves.

Men of great virtue and excellence do not use many formalities; nor do they appreciate or expect that many be used towards them, for they will not waste their thoughts on such vain matters. Neither should workmen and men of low condition be careful to use solemn formalities towards great men and lords because, coming from them, these formalities would be irritating, since it is obedience rather than homage that is expected of them. For this reason the servant errs who makes a show of offering his services to his master, for the master will be offended, thinking that the servant intends to place in doubt his master's lordship over him, suggesting perhaps that he had no right to command and expect obedience.

These kinds of formalities should be freely performed, for what one

---

also because many noble Venetians built villas or acquired estates on the mainland, thus establishing Venetian influences still to be seen in those cities of north-central Italy.

person does out of obligation is received as due and is of little merit to
the one who does it. But he who offers much more than is his duty
seems to be offering something of his own and is loved and considered
generous. And it comes to my mind that I have heard it said that a
worthy Greek, a great poet, used to say that he who knows how to satisfy people with words makes great profit from little capital.[45] Therefore, you will dispense formalities as the tailor produces clothes, that
is, cutting them larger rather than smaller, but not so much that when
you want to make trousers you end up with a sack or a cloak. Therefore, if you use a suitable degree of largesse towards your inferiors you
will be considered courteous; and if you do the same towards your
superiors you will be called a polite gentleman. But the person who is
over-lavish and extravagant with formalities will be accused of being
vain and frivolous and, what is worse, it may happen that he will be
considered a wicked man and a flatterer and, as I hear some literary
men say, a fawning parasite, a vice which our ancients called—if I am
not wrong—unctuousness. No sin is more loathsome or unbefitting
to a gentleman than this one. And this is the third kind of ceremony
which arises from our own will and not from custom.

Let us remember, therefore, that formalities—as I said at the beginning—are not necessary by nature. In fact, one could do without
them, as our nation did until not so very long ago. But someone else's
ills have made us ill with this and many other infirmities. For this reason, once we have obeyed custom and used such permissible lies, anything more is superfluous; however, it is impermissible and forbidden
to go further than custom allows, because formalities then become an
unpleasant and boring thing for men of noble spirit who do not
indulge in such games and pretences.

You must know that when I was planning this treatise, not trusting
in my little knowledge, I consulted with several worthier men of
learning and I found out that a king, whose name was Oedipus, having been banished from his own country sought refuge from the enemies who were pursuing him at the court of Theseus, King of Athens.
As he was about to present himself to the king, Oedipus heard one of
his daughters speak and, recognizing her voice, for he was blind, did
not extend his greetings to Theseus but, as a father would, embraced
the girl. Realizing, then, his error, he wanted to excuse himself with

---

[45]The allusion to the Greek poet is obscure.

the king and ask to be forgiven. But the good and wise Theseus did not allow him to speak and instead said, "Take heart, Oedipus, for I honour my life not with the words of others, but with my own deeds."[46] One must keep in mind this statement. Although men great-ly like to be honoured by others, nevertheless when they are aware that they are being honoured for the sake of mere formality they become weary of it and, furthermore, they disdain it because flattery —or, as I should say, adulation—besides being evil and repulsive, has the additional fault that flatterers openly show that they consider the man they are praising to be vain and arrogant, as well as so stupid and thick-headed and such a simpleton that it is easy to fool him and entrap him. Empty, elaborate, and excessive formalities are but thin-ly disguised adulation. In fact, everybody clearly sees them and recognis-es them as such, so that those who use them for profit, besides being wicked—as I have said above—are also unpleasant and annoying.

[17]

There is another kind of ceremonious person: one who makes an art and a business of it, keeping accounts of ceremonies and setting rules for them. "To one type of person a sneer, and another a smile; and the more honoured person will be offered a chair, the less honoured a bench." I believe such formalities have been brought into Italy from Spain, but our land has received them badly and they have not taken complete hold here, for such a meticulous distinction between degrees of nobility is bothersome to us. Therefore, no one must stand on judg-ment as to who is more or less noble.

Nor should one sell, as harlots do, formalities and praises. This I have seen done by many lords in their courts, who try to give them to their unfortunate servants in lieu of a salary.

And certainly those who take pleasure in using formalities more than is suitable do so out of fickleness and shallowness, like men of little worth. Because such follies are learned very easily and still man-age to make somewhat of a good show, these men learn them very carefully. They cannot learn weightier matters because they are too weak for such a burden; and, not knowing anything better, they would

---

[46]Sophocles, *Oedipus at Colonus*, 3rd episode, lines 1143–44.

like all conversation to be concerned with these frivolities. They have no solid muscle beneath their thin, glossy skin; and if you touch them they are withered and mouldy. For this reason they prefer that all dealings with people not go any deeper than the first impression. And you will find a very great number of such persons.

There are others who exceed in courtly words and deeds in order to make up for the faults of their own wickedness and their uncouth, limited natures, for they are aware that if they were as deficient and rough in words as they are in accomplishments, no one would be able to put up with them.

In truth you will find that for one of these two reasons, and no others, the majority of people abound in the superfluous formalities which generally bother most men. Such habits keep others from living as they wish to live, since their freedom, which is what one seeks above all else, is obstructed.

[18]

One should not speak ill either of other men or of their affairs, even though it is clear that, because of the envy we generally have for other peoples' wealth and honour, ears will gladly stoop to hear it. But in the end everyone flees the charging bull and men avoid the friendship of slanderers because they think that what they said to us about others they also say to others about us.

Some people who contradict every word and always question and argue show that they do not know the nature of men very well, because everyone loves victory and hates defeat both in speech and in action, and also because to contradict others eagerly is a sign of enmity, not friendship. For this reason whoever likes to be a friendly and charming conversationalist must not have a ready, "That's not what happened," or an "On the contrary, it was as I say," nor set up wagers. Instead, he must make an effort to be conciliatory to others in those matters that are of little account. Victory in such cases turns to our detriment for in winning a point in a frivolous question we will often lose a dear friend and become annoying to people, so much so that they dare not deal with us so as not to be constantly arguing. And they nickname us Mister Win-it-all, or Sir Contradiction, or Sir Know-it-all, and sometimes the Subtle Doctor.[47]

---

[47]John Duns Scotus (1266?–1308), called the Subtle Doctor, was educated at

Although it may sometimes happen that someone becomes involved in a dispute at the invitation of those present, this should be done gently and without that thirst for the sweetness of victory that will make the other man choke. Instead, it is proper to let everyone have his say and, whether the opponent is right or wrong, to abide by the opinion of the majority or of the more importunate and leave the field of battle to them, so that others and not you will be the ones to do battle, work hard, and sweat. These are unseemly occupations not suited to well-behaved men, and so one acquires their hatred and dislike. Furthermore, such men are unpleasant because they are unseemly in themselves and thus an annoyance to those with a well-disposed mind, as we will perhaps mention a little later. Most people, however, are so infatuated with themselves that they overlook other people's pleasures; and, in order to show themselves to be subtle, intuitive, and wise, they will advise, and correct, and argue, and contradict vigorously, not agreeing with anything except their own opinions.

To offer your advice without having been asked is nothing else but a way of saying that you are wiser than the man to whom you are giving advice, and even a way of reprimanding him for his limited knowledge and his ignorance. For this reason, it should not be done with everyone you know, but only with the closest friends and with people whom you have the right to rule and guide, or in fact only when someone—even if a stranger to us—is in great and imminent danger. In daily matters, however, one must abstain both from giving advice and from remedying other people's faults. Many fall into these errors, and most often it is the least intelligent, because slow-witted men have little on their minds and so do not spend much time in reaching a decision, like those who do not have many alternatives available to them. Whatever the case, whoever goes about offering and disseminating his advice shows that he is of the opinion that he has more wisdom than he needs and that others lack it. And there are

---

Oxford and Paris and later taught at both universities. Despite his relatively short life, Scotus wrote much and widely and acquired a great reputation. His thought is characterized by subtlety and minute precision. Scotus was a particular target of the humanists, who saw him as the example of everything wrong with medieval scholastic thought (hence Della Casa's reference). Indeed, the English pejorative word "dunce" is derived from Scotus' name.

some who think so highly and with conviction of this wisdom of theirs that not to follow their advice is like wanting to come to blows with them, and they say, "That is fine: a poor man's advice is never taken," and, "So-and-so wants to do as he wants," and, "So-and-so does not listen to me." As if demanding that someone else follow your advice does not show greater arrogance than wanting to follow one's own opinion! A sin similar to this is committed by those who take it upon themselves to correct other men's failings and reprimand them, and want to pass final judgement upon everything and lay down the law to everyone. "Such a thing should not be done." Or, "What a word you have said!" Or, "Stop doing and saying such things." "The wine you drink is not healthy for you. You should drink red wine, instead." Or, "You should use some of this potion, and some of those pills." And they never cease reprimanding or correcting. Not to mention that at times they busy themselves in weeding someone else's garden while their own is full of weeds and nettles. But it is too much bother to listen to them. Just as there are few or no men who could stand to live with their doctor or with their confessor, or even less with a criminal court judge, similarly there are few men to be found who will risk becoming familiar with this type of person because everyone loves freedom and by appearing to be our teachers they deprive us of it. For this reason it is not a pleasant habit to be eager to correct and teach others. This must be left to teachers and fathers. Even from these will sons and students eagerly distance themselves, as you well know.[48]

[19]

One should never mock anyone however great an enemy he may be, because it seems that one shows greater contempt in mocking someone than in doing him wrong. This is so because a man wrongs another man out of anger or out of some covetous desire, and no one is upset by something that he esteems worthless or desires something

---

[48]The irony here, of course, refers to the persona adopted by Della Casa and, indeed, the very purpose of his book. Some levity is introduced to lighten the subject of the book, following the Renaissance humanist dictum of teaching with delight ("docere et delectare").

which he despises completely. So one has some esteem for the man one injures, but none at all or very little indeed for the man one mocks. Mocking consists of taking pleasure, for no personal benefit to ourselves, in the shame we bring on others. Therefore, it is good manners to abstain from mocking anyone. They behave badly who reprove others of some defect either with words, as Messer Forese da Rabatta did when he laughed at Master Giotto's appearance,[49] or with actions, as many do, mimicking those who stutter, or limp, or are hunchbacked. It is also bad manners to laugh at people who are deformed, misshapen, thin or short; or to laugh loudly and make a fuss about a silly thing someone has said; or to take pleasure in making others blush. Such spiteful behaviour is properly detested.

Like these people are the jokers, those who enjoy playing tricks on someone and leading him along not because they want to jest with him or deride him, but simply for the fun of it. You must know that there is no difference between joking and mocking except in purpose and intention; for joking is done for amusement, and mocking is done to hurt. In common speech and writing the two words are often confused, but the difference is that whoever mocks is pleased with the shame he inflicts on another, while he who jokes is not pleased, but rather is amused by the other man's error, and would probably be pained and feel sorry if the other man were made to feel shame. Even though in my youth I did not progress very far with my schooling, I still remember that Micio, who loved Aeschlinus so much that he himself was amazed by it, did nevertheless take pleasure in making fun of him, as when he said to himself: "I am going to play a prank on him."[50] And so the same thing done to the same man can be, depending on the doer's intention, either a joke or a jeer. Since our intention is not easily clear to others, it is not fitting to indulge in practices so unclear and so prone to misunderstanding. One should rather avoid

---

[49]In *Decameron* VI, 5, Forese da Rabatta, who accompanies the painter Giotto on a horse-back voyage through particularly muddy terrain, laughs at him saying that if a stranger were to come upon him and see him so dirty with mud he would never believe that the sullied rider was the best painter in the world. Giotto answers that if the stranger accepted the fact that Forese knew the alphabet he would then have no difficulty in believing that the muddy Giotto was indeed the best painter in the world.

[50]Terence, *Adelphi* IV.5, vv. 696–97.

them than seek to be considered a prankster. Just as it often happens in games and in sports that one man hits another for fun and the other receives the blow as an injury and thus from fun the two men come to blows, so the man who is mocked for fun by a friend will sometimes interpret it as an insult to his honour and will take offence at it. Not to mention that a joke is a deception, and everyone naturally dislikes being wrong and being fooled. It then follows for many reasons that whoever seeks to be well liked and held in high esteem should not make himself a master of pranks.

It is true that we cannot lead this weary mortal life of ours without any recreation or any rest whatsoever, and since jokes do give us reason for some fun and laughter and therefore recreation we like people who are pleasant, humourous, and full of jokes. For this reason the opposite would seem to be true, that is, that it is good manners sometimes to joke and be witty. And certainly those who know how to joke in a friendly and pleasant manner are better liked than those who do not or cannot do so. But it is essential to keep many things in mind when doing so. Since it is the intention of the joker to make fun of an error in someone he respects, the error the other person is made to commit must be such that no noticeable shame or no grave damage could arise from it, otherwise it would be difficult to distinguish jokes from injuries. There are also persons who are so short-tempered that one should under no circumstance poke fun at them, as Biondello found out from Messer Filippo Argenti in the Loggia de' Caviccili.[51]

Similarly, one must not joke about either important or about shameful matters, for, as the saying goes, it seems that one is making fun of sins, although Madonna Filippa da Prato did this to her advantage with the witty answers she gave when questioned about her infidelity.[52]

---

[51] In *Decameron* IX, 8, Ciacco pays Biondello back for a prank he suffered at his hands by arranging things so that the strong, gruff, and very short-tempered Filippo Argenti administers a sound beating on the unsuspecting Biondello.

[52] In *Decameron* VI, 7, Madonna Filippa is caught by her husband in the arms of her lover. At the trial, she manages to have her husband admit that he has always had all he wanted from her. Turning to the judge, she then asks what was she to do with the left-overs? Instead of letting them go to waste, she had, in fact, preferred to donate them to a needy man who also cared for her. Amused by her reply, the judge and the townspeople allowed Filippa to go free.

This is why, in my opinion, Lupo degli Uberti did not lighten his shame but rather aggravated it when he excused himself with a witty remark for the wickedness and cowardice he demonstrated when, though he could safely have held the castle of Laterina, he instead gave it up as soon as he saw it besieged, saying that wolves are not accustomed to being shut up.[53] Puns and light chatter have no place where laughter has no place.

[20]

You must know that there is wit that bites and wit that does not bite. Let Lauretta's wise advice suffice for the former, and that is that wit must bite like a sheep, and not like a dog, for if it bit like a dog it would not be wit but insult.[54] In nearly every city the law is such that whoever insults someone else should be severely punished, and perhaps one should also have ordained no light penalty for anyone who used overly biting witticisms towards someone else. Well-mannered men should consider that the law against slander applies to wit as well, and so mock someone else only rarely and gently at that.

Besides all this, you must realize that unless a witty remark, whether biting or not, is pleasant and subtle, those who hear it will not delight in it. Rather, they will be bored by it or, if they laugh, they will laugh at the "wit" and not at the witticism. Witty remarks are nothing else but deceptions, and deceptions, being subtle and crafty, must be carried out only by astute men with a quick wit, and, above all, unexpectedly. Therefore, they are not suitable to stolid persons with thick heads, nor to anyone with a good, solid head on his shoulders.

---

[53] During the twelfth and thirteenth centuries, the Uberti were a powerful Florentine family. The incident related by the narrator took place in May 1288 when Lupo degli Uberti, perhaps the son of Farinata degli Uberti, was besieged in the castle of Laterina by the Florentine Guelfs. Finding himself surrounded, he surrendered himself punning on his name, "Lupo," which in Italian means "wolf." The description of the incident is taken almost word for word from Giovanni Villani's *Cronache fiorentine* VII, 119–20. For an English translation see *Villani's Chronicle*, trans. Rose E. Selfe and ed. Philip H. Wicksteed (London: Archibald Constable, 1906).

[54] *Decameron* IV, 3.

So, perhaps, they did not befit Messer Giovanni Boccaccio very well. Witty remarks require a special readiness and charm, and immediate mental reactions. For this reason sensible men do not consider their desires, but their aptitude. Having tested in vain the extent of their wit once or twice, and realizing that they are not very gifted, they give up even the desire to exert themselves in this field for fear that they too should suffer what befell Madonna Oretta's knight.[55] If you think about the mode of behaviour of the majority of men, you will easily realize that what I say is true, that wit suits not all those who want to use it, but only those who can use it.

You will see that some men match each word with one or more of those meaningless witticisms we call puns, or switch syllables around within a word in frivolous or silly ways; or answer us in an unexpected manner, with no subtlety or charm, such as:

"Where is he?" "Where his feet are."
"He greased his palms with the oil of St John of the Golden Mouth."[56]
"Where are you sending me?" "To the river"[57]
"I want to shave." "It would be better not to shove."
"Go and call the barber." "What should I call him?"[58]

---

[55] In *Decameron* VI, 1, a gentleman promises to lighten Madonna Oretta's walk in the country by offering her the "horse" of a lively story which he then proceeds to narrate. However, his awkward narrative style soon becomes a nuisance to Oretta, so much so that she points out to the gentleman that his horse has such an uneven trot that she would much rather prefer to walk than to ride. The gentleman, catching her meaning, immediately stops his story.

[56] This is a double pun, referring both to the Florentine coin, the florin, which was inscribed with the image of Saint John the Baptist, Florence's patron saint, and also to the celebrated Patriarch of Constantinople, John Chrysostom (345?–407), whose name in Greek means "of the Golden Mouth." The pun had become proverbial in Florence; see, for example, *Paradiso* XVIII, 133–36, where Dante accuses his fellow Florentines of devotion to St John of the Golden Mouth.

[57] An allusion to the witty remark which Cisti the baker utters in *Decameron* VI, 2 to indicate that the flask Messer Geri's servant wants filled with wine is so big that it would be more suitable for fetching water from the Arno river.

[58] The Italian original puns on the word "barbieri" ("barbers"), extracting the "ieri" ("yesterday") and replacing it with "domani" ("tomorrow").

These, as you can very easily tell, are cheap, low-class witticisms. Such were, for the most part, the pleasantries and puns used by Dioneo.[59]

It is not, however, our task at present to discuss what witticisms are more or less elegant, for there are other treatises on this, written by far better writers and experts than I, and also because witticisms have immediate, extensive and certain proofs of their beauty or of their unpleasantness, and so you will not easily go wrong in this unless you are overly enamoured of yourself.[60] Where a pleasant witticism has been said, there immediately is gaiety, laughter, and a kind of aston-ishment, but where your pleasantries are not rewarded with the laugh-ter of those around you, you will desist from telling witticisms for the fault will be with you and not with your listeners. People are tickled by quick or charming or subtle answers of propositions and even if they try they cannot hold back their laughter and laugh despite them-selves. Your listeners are like a lawful and just jury against whose judg-ment you must not appeal by choosing to make a further trial of yourself based solely on the grounds of your own opinion.

One should not, for the sake of making someone else laugh, say obscene words, or indulge in such ignoble or unsuitable acts as dis-torting one's face and disguising oneself, for no one should debase himself in order to please others. This is the habit not of a gentleman, but of jesters and clowns. The vulgar and low-class manners of Dio-neo are not to be followed when he sang: "Madonna Aldruda, lift your tail."[61] Nor should one pretend to be crazy or foolish, but if he can he should say, at the proper time, something nice and interesting which no one else has thought of, or else keep quiet. For these are matters of the mind, and if they are pleasant and lively they are an indication and a testimonial of the nimble mind and the good habits of the speaker, and this is particularly liked by other men and endears us to

---

[59] Dioneo is one of the narrators in the *Decameron*. At the end of the fifth day, he makes the ladies blush by starting to sing songs whose verses contain sexual double-entendres.

[60] In Book II of Castiglione's *Courtier* there are many jokes recounted for the pleasure of the company. Also, much of Della Casa's advice is found in Cas-tiglione as well.

[61] "Madonna Aldruda, levate la coda, che buone novelle vi reco" is the first of several off-colour songs that Dioneo proposes to sing at the end of day five of the *Decameron*.

them. But if they are without grace and charm, they have the contrary effect and then it seems that an ass is joking, or that someone very fat with an enormous derrière is dancing and hopping about in his shirt-sleeves.

[21]

There is another pleasant kind of speaking, and that occurs when the pleasure lies not in witty remarks which are generally brief, but in a long continuous tale. This must be well arranged, nicely said, and reflect the manners, customs, acts and habits of those of whom one speaks so that the listener will believe not that he is hearing a story but that he is seeing with his own eyes the events you are narrating. Boccaccio's men and women knew very well how to do this, though sometimes, if I am not mistaken, they impersonated the characters more than is suitable for ladies and gentlemen, much like those people who are actors in plays.[62] In order to do this, you must have a clear conception in your mind of the incident, story or event that you undertake to narrate, and the words ready at hand so that you will not find it necessary to say every so often: "That thing" and "That man" or "What's his name?" or "That business" nor "How shall I put it?" and "What did I say his name was?" This was precisely the plodding gait of Madonna Oretta's knight.

If you narrate an event in which many men took part, you must not say "He said" and "He answered," for "he" could be any one of us, and so the listener could easily misunderstand. The narrator must therefore mention the names and then not confuse them.

Furthermore, one should be careful not to include parts which, if left unsaid, make the story no less interesting or, perhaps, even more interesting. "So-and-so, who was the son of the man who lived in Via del Cocomero you knew him, didn't you? His wife was one of the Gianfigliazzi girls? A somewhat thin girl who used to go to mass at San Lorenzo. What do you mean you didn't? Surely you knew him. A fine old man, upright, with hair down to his shoulders, don't you remember him?"[63]

---

[62]Ladies and gentlemen, as Della Casa states throughout *Galateo*, had to maintain the dignity proper to their rank. See also Castiglione's *Courtier* II, p. 113 (Penguin translation).

[63]The frame of reference here is self-consciously Florentine. Real places in

If it did not matter whether the event happened to this man or to another, all this long quibbling would be of little worth—indeed very boring—to the listeners, who are eager and anxious to hear about the event. You would make them wait, as by chance did our Dante, "and my parents were Lombards, both Mantuans by birth,"[64] for it was of no importance if his mother had been from Gazzuolo, or even from Cremona.[65]

In fact, I learnt from a great foreign rhetorician a very useful bit of advice about this, and that is that stories should be thought out and ordered first using nicknames, and then narrated using real names, for the former are given according to a person's character while the latter are given according to the father's pleasure or that of some other such authority.[66] And so that character who in your mind was Lady Avarice in your narration will become Messer Erminio Grimaldi, if the general opinion of him in your neighbourhood is the same as what was said to Guglielmo Borsieri about Messer Erminio of Genoa.[67] If in your city there is not a person similarly well known that would suit your need, you must imagine the event to take place in another city and then give the man whatever name you prefer.

It is certainly true that one listens with more pleasure and one imagines the event more clearly if it involves people we know—given that the event is suited to their manners—than if it is about strangers. This is so because we, knowing that that person is apt to do this,

---

Florence and a real family are described not only to add verisimilitude but also to impress upon young Rucellai (Della Casa's nephew) the immediacy and appropriateness of his advice. The Via Cocomero, in fact, is now the Via Rucellai in Florence. The church of San Lorenzo, which houses the Medici tombs, had its interior redesigned by the Florentine architect Filippo Brunelleschi (1377– 1446).

[64] *Inferno* I, 68–69.

[65] Cremona is a city in Lombardy, about 70 km southeast of Milan. Famous to this day for the string instruments made there, it was later the home of such world-renowned violin makers as the Amati and Stradivarius. Gazzuolo, on the other hand, is a small Lombard town of no particular renown, half-way between Cremona and Mantua.

[66] Such mnemonics had been taught by rhetoricians since classical times. See Frances Yates, *The Art of Memory* (London: Routledge and Kegan Paul, 1966).

[67] In *Decameron* I, 8 Erminio Grimaldi, a miser, was better known by his nickname of Erminio Avarizia (Erminio Avarice). Guglielmo Borsieri was a courtier (d. *c.*1300).

believe that he has done it and we can visualize it, whereas with strangers the same does not occur.

[22]

Both in extended speaking and in other manners of speech, words must be so clear that everyone in the group can understand them with ease, and also beautiful in sound and meaning. And so if you must choose one of these two words, you will rather say "stomach" than "belly," and where your language will bear it you will rather say "tummy" than "belly" or "body" and thus you will be understood, not misunderstood, as we Florentines say, and you will not bring anything unpleasant to your listener's mind.[68] Wanting to avoid such implications in this very word, I believe Petrarch, our most excellent poet, sought to discover another one even if it meant using periphrasis. And so he said: "Remember that our sins made God take on, to save us, human flesh in your virginal cloister."[69]

Because Dante, also a most excellent poet, thought very little about such precepts, I find that little good can be said of him for this reason. I would certainly not advise you to make him your teacher in this art of being elegant, since he himself was not. In fact, in some chronicle I find this written about him: "Because of his knowledge, Dante was presumptuous, scornful, and disdainful, and, lacking in grace, as philosophers are, he did not know very well how to converse with laymen."[70] But to return to our discussion, I say that words ought to be clear; this will be the case if you know how to choose those that are native to your region, and not so ancient that they have become rancid and corrupt and, like worn-out clothes have been cast aside and

---

[68]Because some of the words used by Della Casa as examples are from sixteenth-century Florentine jargon, it is difficult to pin-point precisely the different nuances of the original. Although the English seeks to approximate them, the reader is invited to gather Della Casa's meaning from his general concept rather than from our specific examples.

[69]From Petrarca's canzone "Vergine bella che di sol vestita" (*Canzoniere* CCLXVI, vv. 76–78). The English translation is from *Petrarch's Lyric Poems*, trans. and ed. Robert M. Durling (Cambridge, MA: Harvard UP, 1976).

[70]Giovanni Villani, *Cronache fiorentine* IX, 136.

rejected: for example "spaldo" and "epa" and "uopo" and "sezzaio" and "primaio."[71] Furthermore, the words you use should not have double meanings, but must be simple; for if these ambiguous words are combined one creates that kind of speech which is called enigmatic or, as is said more clearly in the vernacular, a jargon, as for example: "Io vidi un che da sette passatoi / Fu da un canto all'altro trapassato."[72] Your words should also be, as far as possible, appropriate to what you want to demonstrate, and as little applicable to other matters as possible. In this manner it will seem that you are bringing forth the things themselves and that they are being described not with words but with your finger. Therefore it is preferable to say that a man is recognized by his features rather than by his figure or by his image. Dante described the event better when he said "that the weight makes their balances creak thus,"[73] than if he had said either shrieked, screeched, or made a noise. It is more precise to say "the shivers of a fever" than the "cold of a fever;" and "fat meat makes one feel nauseous" rather than "we have had our fill of fatty meat;" and "hang out" the laundry rather than "spread it out;" and "stumps" rather than "severed arms;" and at the edge of a ditch, "the frogs lie...with only the muzzle out"[74] rather than their "mouths." These are all words that have only one meaning. And similarly we should say the "hem" of a cloth rather than the "extremity."

I know very well that if, as my ill luck would have it, a foreigner came across this little treatise of mine he would mock me and say that I was teaching you how to speak in jargon, that is a code, since these words are for the most part particular to our region and no other nation

---

[71]All these words are used by Dante and underline Della Casa's recurring anti-Dantean attitude; "spaldo" (rampart) is found in *Inferno* IX, 133; "epa" (belly) in *Inferno* XXV, 82 and XXX, 102; "uopo" (need, necessity) in *Purgatorio* XVII, 59, in XVIII, 93 and in XXVI, 19; "sezzaio" (last) in *Paradiso* XVIII, 93; "primaio" (first, original) in *Inferno* XXV, 76 and *Purgatorio* XXIX, 145.

[72]There is a play on words with "passotoio" which can mean either a bridge which joins two riverbanks or a projectile which pierces through something. The two verses could thus be interpreted to mean either "I saw a man who was pierced from side to side by seven spears" or "I saw a man who crossed over from side to side by way of seven stepping stones." The verses come from a comic sonnet by Antonio Alamanni, a well-known poet who belonged to the literary circles of mid 16th-century Florence.

[73]*Inferno* XXIII, 101–02.

[74]*Inferno* XXII, 26.

uses them and if it were to use them they would not be understood.[75] And who is there who can know what Dante meant when he said in that verse, "Gia veggia per mezzul perdere o lulla"?[76] I certainly think no one but we Florentines.

Nevertheless, as I have been told, if in that verse of Dante's there is fault to be found, it does not lie with the words. If he went wrong, he went wrong because, being a headstrong man, he undertook to speak about something that is difficult to express in words, and perhaps something that is not pleasant to hear, and not because he expressed it badly.

Therefore, no one can speak effectively with someone who does not understand the language in which he is speaking. If a German does not understand Latin,[77] we must not ruin our own speech when communicating with him, nor engage in mimicry like Master Brufaldo,[78] as do some people who are so foolish as to force themselves to speak in the language of the person with whom they are speaking, whatever it may be, and say everything backwards. It often happens that a Spaniard will speak Italian with an Italian, and the Italian, to show off and to be pleasant, will speak to him in Spanish, and yet it is easier to realize that they are both speaking in a foreign language than to keep from laughing at the silly things that come out of their mouths.

We shall speak then in a foreign language when that is necessary in

---

[75]Given the great geographical, political, linguistic, and cultural diversity present in the Italian peninsula, all of the medieval and Renaissance states saw themselves as separate and quite distinct nations, which of course they were. It is therefore not unusual for Della Casa to imply that the linguistic diversity between Italian regions reflects their different "nationalities." Today we would tend to consider such local linguistic peculiarities as dialectical and cultural variants of one major national group, the Italian one.

[76]As Della Casa says, the verse from *Inferno* XXVIII, 22 is difficult to understand even for Italians because the words are peculiar to the Florentine dialect of the times; "veggia" is a barrel, "mezzule" is the cross-board at the bottom of a barrel, and "lulle" are the crescent-shaped lateral boards at the bottom of a barrel. Sinclair renders this and the following verses into English as "No cask ever gapes by loss of end-board or stave...".

[77]Della Casa really means "Italian", much as Dante refers to Italians as Latins (see, for example, *Inferno* XXVII, 25–26 where Dante refers to Italy as "sweet Latin land"). Peterson translates this passage from Della Casa using the word "Italian," while Pine-Coffin avoids the difficulty by not translating the word at all.

[78]The reference to Master Brufaldo is obscure.

order to make some need of ours understood; but generally let us continue to use our own language, even if inferior, rather than another one, though it may be superior to ours. For a Lombard will speak more properly in his own language, though it is the ugliest dialect of all,[79] than he would in Tuscan or any other because, try as he might, he will never have easily at hand the correct and specific words which we Tuscans have. And if anyone, in order to show consideration for the people with whom he is speaking, seeks to avoid using the local words which I mentioned and in place of them uses generally accepted, standard words, his conversation will thus become much less pleasant.

Every gentleman must also avoid saying indecent words. Decency in words is dependent on their sound, or on their pronunciation, or on their meaning. Some words signify a decent thing, yet one can hear something indecent in pronouncing them, such as "rinculare,"[80] which is nevertheless used daily by everybody. But if anyone, man or woman, were to use some word to mean "to draw forth" coined in the same manner as that word for "to draw back," then the indecency of the word would become apparent. Because of usage, however, our taste for this word perceives its wine rather than its mildew.

"The thief lifted up his hands with both the figs," our Dante said, but our women do not dare say the same.[81] In fact, in order to avoid that suspect word they prefer to say "chestnuts" instead, even though some less careful women often say without thinking that which, if others were to say it casually, would make them blush, since when it is used as an obscenity it describes that which makes them women. Therefore, let those women who are or want to be well mannered take care to avoid not only indecent things but also indecent words, and

---

[79]In their discussions on the ideal Italian language, Italians as far back as Dante compared the different dialects of the peninsula and sought to determine which one came closest to the ideal of a national lan-guage which would be "illustrious, cardinal, courtly and curial" ("illustre, cardinale, aulicum et curiale" *De vulgari eloquentia* I, 17). Dante's conclusion was that no dialect, not even his own Tuscan, was good enough to be used as a standard for the national language (I, 11–16).

[80]"Rinculare" means "to draw back"; "culo" means "ass"; perhaps an English equivalent could be a word such as "assent."

[81]*Inferno* XXV, 2. Della Casa objects to the word "figs" on two counts: it refers to an obscene gesture with the thumb between the index and middle finger, and it is also a very vulgar term for the female genitalia.

not only those that definitely are but also those that could be or could appear to be indecent, vulgar, or coarse, as some say those used by Dante are: "except for the wind blowing in my face and from below";[82] or else these: "tell us again where the opening is at hand...and one of those spirits said 'Come behind us and thou shalt find the gap.'"[83] You must realize that although two or more words may come to mean the same thing, none the less one will be more decorous and the other less so. And so one should say, "She lay with him," or, "She satisfied him with her person," because this idea, said with other words, would be an indecent thing to hear. It would be more polite for you to say "her heart's desire" rather than "paramour," even though both these words mean "lover."[84] It seems to be a more acceptable manner of speech to say the "girl" or the "friend" rather than the "mistress of Tithonus."[85] It is better manners for a lady and even for a gentleman to call prostitutes "women of the world," as Belcolore,[86] who had more shame in her speech than in her actions, said than to use the name commonly given them, as in, "It is Thais, the whore."[87] Thus Boccaccio said, "the power of prostitutes and boys,"[88] for he would have been vulgar and shameful in his speech had he used for the boys, as he had for the women, a term based on their profession.

In fact, one should not only refrain from indecent and obscene words, but also from base words, especially where one speaks of high and noble matters. For this reason, perhaps, Beatrice deserved some blame when she said: "God's high decrees would be broken if Lethe

---

[82] *Inferno* XVII, 117.

[83] *Purgatorio* XVIII, 111, 113–14.

[84] The original Italian, "il vago della luna," is a Petrarchan image (*Canzoniere* CCXXXVII, 3). Pine-Coffin translates it as "a lady's favorite," and Peterson renders it with "Endymion." Peterson's translation actually names the mythical character referred to by the Italian and by this translation. Endymion was a shepherd of surpassing beauty whom the moon goddess Selene, falling in love with him, made fall into a magic, eternal slumber. Every night, as he sleeps, she descends from the heavens to caress him and cover him with kisses.

[85] *Purgatorio* IX, 1.

[86] In *Decameron* VIII, 2, Monna Belcolore, before lying with her village priest, asks him for five lire; when he claims not to have such money on him, she settles for his cloak of fine Turkish cloth as payment for her services.

[87] *Inferno* XVIII, 133.

[88] *Decameron* I, 2.

were passed and such a draught were tasted without some scot of penitence."[89] In my opinion, the base word appropriate to an inn did not fit in such a noble discussion. Nor should one say "the lamp of the world" in place of "the sun" because for some persons such a word implies the stink of oil and of the kitchen.[90] Nor would any prudent man say that Saint Dominic was the "lover" of theology,[91] nor would he say that the glorious saints had uttered such base words as: "and then let them scratch where it itches,"[92] words that are sullied with the filth of the common people, as anyone can readily ascertain.

Therefore, when you speak at length you must consider those things mentioned above and some others which you may easily learn from your teachers and from the art that they call Rhetoric. In other manners of speech you must accustom yourself to using words that are polite, simple and sweet, so that there is no bitter flavour to your language. You will sooner say, "I did not explain myself well," rather than, "You do not understand me"; and, "Let us just consider if we are interpreting things correctly," rather than, "You are wrong," or, "That is not true," or, "You do not know." It is a polite and pleasant habit to excuse a man's fault even when you know him to be in the wrong. In fact, one should share a friend's own error and first claim a portion of it oneself, and then reprove him for it and correct him. You should say, "We have taken the wrong road" and "Yesterday we did not remember to do this," even though it was your friend alone who was forgetful, and not you. What Restagnone said to his companions was not right: "You, if your words do not lie …"[93] because it is not proper to question other people's good faith. In fact, if someone promised you something and did not deliver, it is not correct for you to say,

---

[89] *Purgatorio* xxx, 142–45. Della Casa objects to the word "scot," which is the term used for payment made to an innkeeper and therefore is inappropriate to this context.

[90] The original Italian word "Lanterna" meant "light" in Dante's time, hence Della Casa's objection is invalid because he did not catch the true thirteenth-century meaning of the word.

[91] The phrase is uttered by Saint Bonaventure as he talks to Dante about Saint Domenic (*Paradiso* xii, 55). In Dante's verse the word is also modified by the adjective "amoroso" ("loving"), which would further strengthen Della Casa's objection to such a description of Saint Domenic.

[92] *Paradiso* xvii, 129.

[93] *Decameron* iv, 3.

"You did not keep your word," unless you are forced to say it by some necessity, for the safeguarding of your honour, for example. If someone has deceived you, you should sooner say: "You did not remember to do this"; and if he did not remember you should sooner say, "You could not do it," or, "It slipped your mind," rather than "You forgot," or, "You did not care to keep your promise to me," because such words have the sting and poison of protest and spite in them. Because of this, those people who make it a habit to use such words often are considered to be mean and rough fellows, and one avoids their company as much as one avoids becoming tangled up in thorns and thistles.

[23]

I have known some people who have that bad and irritating habit of being so eager and anxious to say something that they fail to make their point and, instead, overtake it and run ahead of it like a greyhound who cannot catch his quarry. I must, therefore, tell you what may seem unnecessary to bring to your attention because it is obvious, and this is that you must never speak unless you have first thought out in your mind what you are going to say. In this manner your arguments will be well delivered and not miscarry at birth—and any stranger reading this idle chat of mine will permit me to use this image. If you take my teachings seriously, you will never find yourself saying, "Welcome, Messer Agostino" to someone whose name is Agnolo or Bernardo; and you will not be forced to say: "What was your name, again?"; or say over and over again, "I did not express myself clearly" or "How shall I put it," or stammer and stutter at length in order to remember a word. It is like being put on the rack to have to listen to someone say: "Master Arrigo—oh, no. Master Arabico. That's it! Master Agapito."

One's voice should be neither hoarse nor shrill. One should not shriek, nor squeak like a pulley-wheel because of laughter or some other reason. Nor should someone speak while yawning. You know very well that we cannot acquire a smooth tongue or a good voice at will, so anyone who stutters or croaks should not be the one who is always chattering away. Instead, he should correct the defect of his tongue through silence and listening, and he can also improve this fault of nature by practising. It is not proper to raise one's voice like a town crier, nor should one speak so softly that the listener cannot hear. If at first you have not been heard, you must not speak even more softly the second time around nor should you shout so as to show that you are becoming irritated at having to repeat what you have said.

Words must be arranged according to the demands of common speech, not convoluted or complicated here and there, as many speakers are wont to do whimsically. The speech of these people is more like that of a notary translating into Italian the documents he dictated in Latin rather than that of a man who is conversing in his own native tongue.[94] To say things such as, "following after false images of good,"[95] and "these temples are blossoming white before their time,"[96] may sometimes be suitable to someone who is writing verses, but are always unsuitable to someone who is speaking.

In speaking, a man should avoid sounding like a versifier and also avoid the pomposity of a public speaker. Otherwise, he will be unpleasant and tedious to hear, even though a public discourse may show greater mastery of speech than informal speaking does. There is a time and a place for that. A man on the street should walk, not dance, even though everyone knows how to walk but not everyone knows how to dance. Dancing is appropriate at weddings, not in the streets. You will therefore avoid pompous speech such as: "It is believed by many philosophizers …"[97] as well as the entire *Filoloco* and the other treatises by Messer Giovan Boccaccio (except for his major work, the *Decameron* and, perhaps even more than that one, the *Corbaccio*).[98]

I want you, however, to become accustomed not to the base speech of the dregs of the populace like the washer-woman and the street-hawker, but to that of gentlemen instead. I have partly shown you

---

[94] Notaries wrote legal documents for a fee, keeping a copy as a record. Here Della Casa is referring to the halting style resulting from oral, sight translation into the vernacular of the official document written in Latin.

[95] *Purgatorio* xxx, 131.

[96] From Petrarca's sonnet "Non da l'ispano Ibero a l'indo Idaspe" (*Canzoniere* ccx, v. 14).

[97] This is the particularly pompous beginning of a speech by Titus Quintus Fulvius, who studied philosophy at Athens (*Decameron* x, 8).

[98] One of Boccaccio's early and minor works, the *Filocolo* is a novel describing the love between Florio and Biancifiore. The *Corbaccio*, again a minor work, is a misogynistic and satiric work.

above how this can be done, that is, you must not speak of low things, or frivolous, gross, or disgusting ones. You must know how to choose among the words of your language those that are purest and most appropriate and those with the best sound and meaning, without any insinuation of anything ugly, dirty, or low, and put them together without piling them up randomly or stringing them together with undue and obvious artifice. And besides this you must seek to arrange your thoughts judiciously, and beware of juxtaposing things that are incompatible, such as "Cicero, Linus and Seneca the moralist,"[99] or "One was a Paduan, the other a layman."[100]

You must not speak slowly, as if you were lazy, nor avidly, as if you were famished; but you must speak as a sober man should. You must pronounce syllables and sounds with suitable grace, not like a schoolmaster who is teaching children how to read and write. Nor should you chew your words, or swallow them all joined and pasted together. If you will thus keep in mind these and other similar rules, people will eagerly and pleasantly listen to you when you speak and you will maintain the degree and dignity proper to a well brought-up and well mannered gentleman.

[24]

There are also many people who cannot stop speaking. Just as a ship driven by its force does not stop when the sails are furled, so these people driven by some momentum run on and, having exhausted their argument, still do not stop but rather continue idly or repeat what they have already said.

Others are so avid to speak that they do not allow others to say anything. Just as we sometimes see in a farmyard a chicken take a grain away from another's beak, so these men take the words out of the mouth of the man who began to talk and speak them themselves. They surely make the other person eager to come to blows with them

---

[99] *Inferno* IV, 141. Della Casa objects to associating a character from mythology (Linus) with the great Roman orator Marcus Tullius Cicero (106–43 B.C.) and the Roman rhetorician Seneca (4 B.C.–65 A.D.).

[100] From the sonnet "Io vidi un dì" (v. 12) of the Florentine barber and burlesque poet Domenico di Giovanni, called il Burchiello (1404–49).

because, if you observe, nothing moves a man to anger more quickly than when his desire and pleasure, no matter how small, is suddenly ruined, as for example when someone shuts your mouth with his own hands just when you had begun to open it in order to yawn, or when someone suddenly holds your arm from behind just when you had raised it to throw a stone.

Therefore, just as these and many other similar manners which tend to obstruct other people's wishes and pleasures are unpleasant and ought to be avoided even if done for fun or in sport, so in speaking one should ease rather than obstruct other people's wishes. Therefore, if someone is ready to tell a story it is not suitable to ruin it for him nor to tell him that you already know it. And if he inserts in his story some small lie, he should not be reproved for it either in words or by such actions as shaking one's head or giving him a dirty look. People often do this claiming that they cannot stand under any circumstance the bitterness of lies, but this is not so. On the contrary, it is the sharpness and sourness of their own rough and quarrelsome nature that renders them so spiteful and bitter in the company of others that no one can abide them. Similarly, to interrupt someone as he is speaking is an irritating and unpleasant habit, not unlike that of holding back a man who is ready to run.

Nor is it suitable to leave or ignore a man when he is speaking, or to point out to his listeners some other thing, or lead their attention somewhere else, for it is not proper of anyone to dismiss a person whom someone else, and not he, has invited.

You should pay attention to someone who is speaking so that you will not have to say, again and again: "Eh?" or "What?" Many people have this fault, and it is no less a nuisance to a speaker than tripping over a rock is to a person who is walking. All these habits and generally all those which can stop or interrupt the course of another man's speech are to be avoided.

If anyone is slow in his speech, one should not get ahead of him or lend him words, as if you had a surplus and he lacked a few. Many people take this badly, especially those who have persuaded themselves that they are good speakers; for they then believe that you do not have the same opinion of them as they have of themselves and that you want to help them at their own craft, much as merchants take offence if others lend them money, as if they did not have enough themselves and were poor and needed other people's help. You must realize that everyone believes he can speak well, even though for modesty's sake everyone denies it.

I cannot guess why it is so, but those who know the least speak the most. Well-mannered men should guard themselves against this, that is, from speaking too much, especially if they know little, not only because it is an amazing thing if one can speak a lot without making many mistakes, but also because it seems that he who speaks stands over those who listen, like a teacher over his pupils. Therefore, it is not proper to appropriate a greater portion of this superiority than befits any single person. Not only many men but also many chattering and prattling nations fall into this sin, and woe be to the ears they seize upon.

Just as speaking too much is a nuisance, so keeping too silent is irritating, for to keep quiet where others are engaged in conversation seems to show an unwillingness to pay one's share of the bill. Because speaking is a way of opening your soul to your listener, to keep quiet seems to imply, on the contrary, a willingness to want to remain a stranger. For this reason, just as in some countries where people drink a lot at their feasts and get drunk it is the custom to throw out those who do not drink, so this type of mute fellow is not eagerly welcomed in cheerful and friendly company. It is a pleasant habit, therefore, for each to speak and to keep quiet when it is his turn.

[25]

According to a very ancient chronicle, there once lived in Morea[101] a good man, a sculptor by trade, who was so clear-headed that he was nicknamed, as I believe, Clearest.[102] Because he was already of an advanced age, this man wrote a treatise in which he gathered up all the rules of his craft with the authority of someone who had known them very well. He showed how the limbs of the human body ought to be measured, each independently and each in relation to the others so that

---

[101] Morea is the medieval name for the Peloponnese, the major peninsula in Greece, and an area once part of the Venetian maritime empire.

[102] Polycleitus, which in Greek means "very clear" (480–405 B.C.). Aristotle mentions him and Phidias in the *Ethics*, Bk VI, c. 7. In classical times he is also mentioned by Cicero, Galen and Pliny; in the Middle Ages by Dante (*Purgatorio* X, 32–35).

they should be in proper proportion among themselves. He called this volume his *Canon*, meaning that henceforth every master of the craft should shape and design statues according to it, just as beams, stones, and walls are measured with a standard ruler. But the fact is that things are more easily said than done. Also, most men, and especially laymen and uneducated persons like me, are always readier with the senses than with the intellect; therefore, we learn better through specific examples than through general principles and syllogisms (which in the clearer vernacular tongue must mean the reasons). So the above-mentioned good man, having seen the type of people these sculptors were—that is, not well disposed to general rules—and in order to demonstrate even more clearly his own expertise, provided himself with a fine block of marble. And after long, hard work he carved a statue from it that was as regular in each of its limbs and in each of its parts as his treatise proposed in its rules. And he called the statue "The Canon," just like the book.

Now may it be God's pleasure that I may do, at least in part, one of the two things that this excellent sculptor and teacher was able to do perfectly: that is, to put together in this volume the proper measures, so to speak, of the craft which I am discussing. It is too late for me to carry on with the other part and actually compose the second "Canon," which would be to live by and illustrate in my habits the above-mentioned rules, making of them a visible example, like the actual statue. This is so because in matters dealing with manners and customs of men it is not enough to know the theory and the rule, it is also necessary, in order to put them into effect, to practise them. This cannot be accomplished in a moment or in a short period of time, but should be done over many, many years. As you can see, I have very few years left now. But you should not place less faith in these teachings because of this; for a man can well teach others to follow that road in which he took many wrong turns. In fact, those who lost their way can perhaps remember better the misleading and dubious paths than the man who always kept to the right road.

If in my youth, when I was pliable and impressionable, those who cared about me had known how to bend my habits, which were perhaps somewhat hard and rough by nature, and had softened and polished them, I could perhaps have become a man such as I am now trying to make of you who are to me no less dear than a son. Although the forces of nature are great, nevertheless they are often over-come and corrected by custom. But it is necessary to begin to resist them early, and to control them before they become too powerful and bold. The majority of people, however, do not do this and instead are misled by their instincts, following them without resistance wherever they may lead. They thus believe they are obeying their natures as if reason were not natural to men. On the contrary, reason is lord and master: she has the power to change corrupt habits and assist and raise up nature whenever, from time to time, it slips or falls. For the most part, however, we do not listen to our reason and so most of the time we are similar to beasts, to whom God did not grant reason. Yet, reason has some power over these animals; not their own reason, for they have none, but ours. This you can see in horses who often—in fact always—would by nature be wild unless their tamer rendered them meek and, more than this, almost wise and well-behaved. For although many such animals would proceed in a hard trot, he teaches them to proceed with a light step, to stay, to run, to turn, and to jump; and they learn it, as you know they do.

Now, if horses, dogs, birds, and many other animals wilder still than these submit to someone else's reason and obey it contrary to their nature and become almost docile and prudent, to the extent that their condition allows it, how much better, we believe, would we become if we lent an ear to the teachings of our own reason? But the senses love and lust for immediate pleasures, whatever they may be, and they abhor bothersome things and put them off. And so they avoid reason as well, which seems bitter to them, for it often presents them not with pleasure, which is often harmful, but with their own good, which always requires an effort and tastes bitter to the still corrupted palate. Thus, while we still live according to the senses we are like a pitiful invalid to whom every dish, no matter how refined and exquisite, seems bitter and salty. He then complains about the servant-girl or the cook, who is not at all to blame for this, for in fact he is tasting his own bitterness, of which his tongue is full, and does not taste the food itself. Thus, reason, which is sweet in itself, seems bitter to us not because of its taste, but because of ours. Being delicate and spoiled, we therefore refuse to taste it and excuse our faintheartedness by saying that nature knows no spur or rein that can drive her on or hold her back. Surely if bulls, or donkeys, or perhaps pigs could talk, I do not think they could utter a much fouler or more inept statement than this one.

We would still be children both in our mature years and in our old age, and we would still be playing when our hair has turned grey with age as we did when we were toddlers were it not for reason which grows in us with our years. And, grown up, it makes us men where before we were nearly beasts. Thus, she has power over the senses and the instincts, and it is our wickedness, not her fault, if we go amiss in our lives and in our habits. It is therefore not true that against nature there is neither rein nor master.[103] On the contrary, there are two of them: one is good manners, the other reason. But, as I have said to you shortly before, without good manners which are a child and a product of time, reason cannot make an uncouth man into a courteous one.

Consequently, one should begin to listen to reason early on, not only because a man thus has a longer period of time in which to become accustomed to follow her teachings and become her servant and be one of her train, but also because youth in its purity takes on colours more easily; and also those things to which one first grows accustomed always tend to be more pleasing. For this reason it is told that Diodato,[104] a great master in reciting comedies, always wanted his own play to be staged first, in spite of the fact that those who were to come before him were not highly thought of, because he did not want his voice to find the ears of his spectators accustomed to other voices, even though they would have been worse than his.

Since, for the reasons I have told you, I cannot suit my deeds to my words as did Master Clearest, who knew how both to do and to teach, let it suffice for me to have said at least in part what one should do; for I am unfit to put any part of it into practice. But just as in seeing darkness one learns what light is, and in hearing silence one learns what sound is, so also you will be able to perceive, in looking at my poor and uncouth manners, what the light of pleasant and praise-worthy manners may be. Returning to the discussion of these manners, which will shortly come to an end, let us say that pleasant manners are those

---

[103]The senses were viewed as lower than the understanding of the mind and as part of our animal nature, whereas reason was the special gift of God to mankind alone. These ideas were essentially from the Greek, a philosophical heritage common to so many major Renaissance writers, including Castiglione, Michelangelo, Poliziano, and Ficino.

[104]Theodorus was a Greek actor of the 4th century. His name is Italianized to maintain the feigned ignorance of the speaker. See Castiglione's *Courtier* II, 8.

which delight or at least do not irritate any of the senses, the desires or the imagination of those with whom we are dealing. It is about these things that we have talked till now.

[26]

You must also realize that men are very desirous of beauty, measure, and proportion. Conversely, men detest things that are ugly, unnatural, and mis-shapen. This is a special quality in men, for the other animals do not know how to recognize any degree of beauty or proportion. Therefore, since beauty, measure, and proportion are things which we do not have in common with beasts but are peculiar to us, we must appreciate them in themselves and hold them very dear. This is especially true of those men who have greater sensitivity for they are more apt to come to know them. And although it is difficult to express precisely what beauty is, nevertheless, so that you may have some indication of what beauty is, I want you to know that, where there is suitable proportion among the parts in themselves and between the parts and the whole, there beauty lies.[105] Something may truly be called beautiful if that proportion I mentioned is found in it.

According to what I have heard before from a wise and learned man, beauty has unity, as much as possible; and ugliness, instead, multiplicity. Such, as you can see, are the faces of beautiful and pretty young girls, for the features of each appear to have been created for one face alone. This does not happen in the case of an ugly girl, for if by chance she has very large and prominent eyes, a small nose, puffed-out cheeks, a thin mouth, a protruding chin, or dark skin, it seems that her face does not belong to one woman alone, but is composed from the faces of many women and is made up of different parts.

Some women can be found whose different parts, each on its own, are very beautiful to the eyes, but put together they are unpleasant

---

[105] Della Casa adheres to the Ciceronian definition: "physical beauty with harmonious symmetry of the limbs engages the attention and delights the eye" (*De officiis*, trans. Walter Miller, Loeb Classical Library (London: William Heinemann, 1928), I.xxviii.98). Cicero gives another definition in the *Tusculane* IV, 13, which is the one Agnolo Firenzuola (c.1493–1545), another of Della Casa's friends, mentions when he says: "In his *Tusculane* Cicero says that beauty consists

and ugly for no other reason but that they are the features of several
beautiful women but not of the one in particular who seems to have
borrowed them from this or that girl. Perhaps that painter for whom
Calabrian girls posed nude did nothing more than recognize in many
of those girls the limbs which each one had acquired from one original
woman's body. Once each girl had returned the borrowed limb to that
original body he set himself to paint it, believing Venus' beauty to be
such and so proportioned.[106]

I do not want you to think that this is true only for bodies and
faces. In fact, it happens just as much in speech and behaviour. If you
saw a well-dressed noblewoman washing her dirty dishes in the gutter
at the roadside, you would be disappointed with her inconsistency,
even if you did not otherwise care for her. Her appearance would be
that of an elegant noble lady, but her behaviour would be that of a
low serving woman. Even if there were no harsh odour or taste from
her, nor any irritating sound or colour, nor anything else about her
that should trouble your senses, you would still be displeased by that
unpleasant, unbefitting and unsuitable act.

[27]

You must therefore be just as wary of this disorderly and unsuitable
behaviour as of those things of which I have spoken so far. In fact,
more so. It is more difficult to know when one errs in these actions
than in those since it is plainly easier to see than to understand. Never-the-
less, it can often happen that whatever displeases the senses displeases

---

of a suitable arrangement of parts with a certain softness of colour"(*On the Beauty
of Women*, trans. Konrad Eisenbichler and Jacqueline Murray (Philadelphia: U of
Pennsylvania P, 1992), 13–14). The Renaissance locus classicus of this concept
of beauty as harmony and proportion was the *De pictura* by the Florentine Leon
Battista Alberti (1404–72), supported and refined by his writings on architec-
ture and sculpture.

[106]Zeuxis of Heraclea (d. 397 B.C.), a Greek painter, was celebrated mostly for
his depiction of the female form. Pliny, Lucian, and Cicero tell many curious anec-
dotes concerning him. Della Casa is mistaken when he says that Zeuxis sought to
portray Venus in this fashion: in fact it was Helen, and it was done for the Temple
of Hera on the Lacinian promontory of Magna Graecia. The error is common.

the intellect as well, but not for the same reasons, as I explained earlier when I said that a man should dress according to the custom of others so as not to show that he is reprimanding them or correcting them. This displeases the feelings of the majority of people because they like to be praised. But this is also offensive to the judgment of discerning men, for the clothes of another age do not go well with a man of our times.

By the same token those people who buy their clothes second-hand are also displeasing, for their garments fit so badly that their doublets clash with their hose. Many of the things we spoke about before, and perhaps all of them, could quite rightly be repeated here, because they do not observe that decorum we are now discussing, nor are the time, the place, the deed and the person all co-ordinated and unified, as they should be. The intellect of men appreciates and takes great plea-sure and delight in harmony. But I preferred to gather them up and arrange them according to that heading, so to speak, of senses and desires, rather than assign them to the intellect so that everyone might recognize them more easily. Everyone experiences feelings and desires quite easily, but not everyone can do the same with understanding, especially when dealing with those things we call beautiful, pretty, and attractive.

[28]

Therefore, a man must not be content with doing what is good, but he must also seek to do it gracefully. Grace is nothing else but some-thing akin to a light which shines from the appropriateness of things that are suitably ordered and arranged one with the other, and in rela-tion to the whole. Without this measure, even that which is good will not be beautiful, and beauty will not be pleasing. Just as with food, which though wholesome and nutritious will not please the guests if it has a bad taste or no taste at all, so it will sometimes be with a man's manners. Even if there is nothing harmful in them, they will appear silly or distasteful unless he flavours them with that certain sweetness which is called, as I believe, grace or charm.

For this reason alone, every vice must be in itself offensive to other people, for vices are such ugly and improper things that their unsuit-ability displeases and disturbs every sober and well-balanced spirit.

Therefore, it is most advisable for those who aspire to be well liked in dealing with other people to flee vices, especially the fouler ones such as lust, avarice, cruelty, and the like. Some of these vices are despicable, such as gluttony or drunkenness; some are filthy, such as being a lecher; some are evil, such as murder. Similarly, other vices are despised by people, some more than others, each for its own nature and quality. But, as I have shown you before, all vices in general, because they are disordered things, render a man unpleasant in the company of others. However, since I undertook to show you men's errors and not their sins, my present care must be to deal not with the nature of vice and virtue, but only with the proper and improper manners we use toward each other. One of these improper manners was the one used by Count Ricciardo, of whom I told you above.[107] It was so different from and discordant with his other beautiful and fitting manners that the worthy bishop immediately noticed it, as a good and well trained singer notices wrong notes.

It is therefore suitable for well-mannered persons to be mindful of this balance of which I have spoken in their walking, standing, sitting, movements, bearing, and in their dress, in their words, in their silence, in their repose, and in their actions. Thus, a man must not embellish himself like a woman, for his adornments will then contradict his person, as I see some men do, who put curls in their hair and beards with a curling iron, and who apply so much make-up to their faces, necks, and hands that it would be unsuitable for any young wench, even for a harlot who is more anxious to hawk her wares and sell them for a price.

One should not smell either foul or sweet, so that a gentleman does not smell like a beggar or a man like a common woman or a harlot. Still, I do not say that at your age certain simple fragrances made from distilled waters are not suitable. For the reasons I have mentioned above, your clothes should be according to the custom of those like you in age and condition. We do not have the power to change customs as we see fit, for it is time that creates them and likewise it is time that destroys them. Everyone, however, may adapt the current fashion to his own need. For example, if your legs are very long and the fashion calls for short clothes, you could make your garments a little less short. If someone has very thin legs, or unduly fat ones, or perhaps crooked ones, he should not wear hose of bright or attractive colours so as not to invite others to gaze at his defect.

---

[107] See Chapter 4.

Your garments should not be extremely fancy or extremely ornate, so that no one can say that you are wearing Ganymede's hose,[108] or that you have donned Cupid's doublet. But whatever clothes you are wearing should fit your body well and suit you, so that it does not look as if you are wearing someone else's clothing. And above all they must befit your condition, so that a priest does not look like a soldier, or the soldier like a jester.[109] When Castruccio[110] was in Rome with Louis the Bavarian[111] and enjoyed the glory and pomp of being duke of Lucca and Pistoia, count of Palazzo, a senator of Rome, lord and master at the court of the aforementioned Bavarian, he had made, for his pleasure and ostentation, a cloak of crimson velvet which on the breast bore in golden letters the motto "It is as God wills" and on the back, in similar letters, "It shall be as God wills." I believe you will recognize that this cloak would have been more appropriate for Castruccio's trumpeter than for Castruccio himself. And, although kings are above the law, still I could not commend King Manfred for the fact that he always dressed in green.[112]

We must therefore take care that our garments fit not only the body but also the status of the person who wears them. And, furthermore, they should be suitable to the place where we live. For as in other lands there are other weights and measures and yet one sells, buys, and trades in every country, so in different places there are different customs and yet in every land a man can behave and dress himself properly.

---

[108]Ganymede was a very beautiful young Trojan boy whom Zeus carried off to Olympus to serve as cup-bearer to the gods.

[109]Della Casa may have had in mind Pope Julius II, who often donned armour and personally led his troops into battle, or Titian's portrait of Cardinal Ippolito de' Medici in a Hungarian hunting costume. Such excesses were more typical of the earlier part of the century; by Della Casa's time they had been restrained by the changed religious climate.

[110]Castruccio Castracani (1281–1328), a famous condottiere created duke of Lucca in 1327. For the description of the cloak see Villani, *Cronica* x, 60. Machiavelli wrote a biography of Castruccio.

[111]Louis IV, called the Bavarian, crowned emperor in Rome in January 1328.

[112]Manfred (1232–66), natural son of the emperor Frederick II Höhenstaufen, was king of Sicily and Apulia (1254–66). He died at the battle of Benevento fighting against the invading forces of Charles of Anjou, and his body was never found. When Dante meets Manfred in Purgatory, the king tells how

The feathers that Neapolitans and Spaniards wear on their hats, and their elaborate trimmings and embroideries, do not suit the apparel of serious men or the clothes of city-dwellers. Armour and chain-mail are even less suitable. So, what is perhaps suitable in Verona in Venice may not do,[113] for these men, so feathered, decorated, and armed are out of place in that venerable city of peace and orderliness.[114] In fact, they appear like nettles and burrs among good and sweet garden greens, and for this reason are ill received in noble gatherings, because they are so out of keeping with them.

A noble man must not run in the street, nor hurry too much, for this is suitable for a groom and not for a gentleman. Besides, a man will tire himself out, sweat and pant for breath, all of which are unbecoming to men of quality. Nor, on the other hand, should one proceed as slowly or demurely as a woman or a bride does. Also, it is unsuitable to wiggle too much when walking. One should not let his arms dangle, nor swing them around, nor throw them about so that it looks like he is sowing seed in a field. Nor should one stare a man in the face as though there was something to marvel at.

There are some who, when walking, lift their feet high up, like a frightened horse, and it looks as if they are pulling their legs out of a bushel basket. Others stamp their feet so hard on the ground that they make almost as much noise as a cart. One man points out with one of his feet. Another man raises one leg more than the other. There are some men who bend over at every step to pull up their stockings, and some who wiggle their behinds and strut like peacocks. These things are unpleasant not because they are very appealing, rather quite the opposite.

If by chance your horse held his mouth open or showed its tongue, even though it would not reflect on its skills, it would affect its price very much and you would get very much less for it, not because this

---

his enemies dug up his body and left it unburied by the shores of the Liri river which, swollen by the rains, eventually carried it away (*Purgatorio* III, 103–14).

[113]Since 1405 Verona had been under the dominion of Venice. Previously, the city had been ruled by princes (*signori*), and thus enjoyed different social traditions from republican, maritime Venice.

[114]During the Renaissance, Venice was seen as the great example of a peaceful, orderly, well governed city. Many Florentine humanists wrote praises of the Venetian system of aristocratic, republican rule in which all citizens seemed to be content.

habit would make him less strong, but because it would make him less graceful. We also see that two equally well built and comfortable houses will not have the same price if one appears well proportioned and the other does not. Thus, if one appreciates grace in animals and even in things, which have no soul or feelings, how much more should one seek and appreciate it in men?

[29]

It is impolite to scratch oneself while at table. At that time a man should also as much as possible avoid spitting; but if he must he should do it discreetly. I have often heard it said that there have been countries so sober that their inhabitants never spat.[115] We can certainly refrain from it for a short time.

We must also be careful not to gobble up our food and develop hiccups or some other unpleasant result, as happens with people who hurry and so gasp for air or breathe so heavily that they annoy their companions.

Similarly, it is not proper to rub one's teeth with one's napkin, and even less with one's finger, for these are unsightly acts. Nor is it proper to rinse one's mouth with wine and then spit it out in public. And it is not a polite habit to carry a toothpick in one's mouth when getting up from the table, like a nesting bird, or to keep it tucked behind the ear like a barber.

Those who carry their toothpicks tied to a chain around their neck are certainly at fault. Besides being a strange tool for a gentleman to be seen extracting from his shirt, it reminds us of those tooth-pullers we see standing on benches to extract teeth in public. It also shows that that person is well equipped and prepared for the service of his gluttony. And I cannot tell exactly why these men do not carry a spoon as well tied to a chain around their necks.

It is also unsuitable to sprawl over the table, or to fill both sides of your mouth with food until your cheeks puff out. Also, you must not

---

[115]This is an allusion to the Persians. Xenophon, whom the learned Della Casa would have read, writes: "for even to the present time it is a breach of decorum for a Persian to spit or to blow his nose or to appear afflicted with flatulence." (*Cyropaedia*, trans. Walter Miller, Loeb Classical Library (London: William Heinemann, 1968), 1.ii.16).

do anything that shows someone else how greatly you are enjoying the food or the wine, for these are habits for the taverns and for drunkards.[116]

To encourage those who are at table with you with words such as "Are you not eating, this morning?" or, "Is there nothing that you like?" or, "Taste some of this or some of that" does not seem to me to be praiseworthy, even though the majority of people believe it is friendly and acceptable. Although in so doing they show concern for their guest, very often they are also the reason why he eats so sparingly, for it will seem to him that he is being carefully watched and will be embarrassed. I do not believe that it is proper to offer something from one's own plate unless the person who is offering it is of a much more exalted rank; then the person who receives it will consider this an honour. Between men of equal rank, it will seem that the person who is offering is somehow making himself the superior of the one to whom he is offering it, and sometimes what is given may not be to the other person's taste. Besides, this shows that the banquet does not have sufficient dishes and that they are not evenly distributed, for one person has too much and another not enough, and this could embarrass the master of the house. Nevertheless, in this matter we must do what is done, and not what should be done, for it is better to be impolite with others than to be correct all by oneself. But whatever is proper, you must not refuse what is offered to you for it will seem that you either despise or rebuke the man who is offering it to you.

It is also a barbarous habit to challenge someone to a drinking bout. This is not one of our Italian customs and so we give it a foreign name, that is "brindisi."[117] It has not yet become the practice in our lands and so it should not be done. If someone should invite you to a drinking bout, you can easily refuse the invitation and say that you admit defeat, thanking him and tasting the wine out of courtesy, without drinking more of it.

Still this "brindisi," as I have heard it claimed by several learned men, may have been an ancient custom in certain parts of Greece.

---

[116]The original says "Cinciglioni," which is a reference to *Decameron* I, 6, where a fellow by the name of Cinciglione is characterized as a drunkard.

[117]From the Spanish "brindar," which in turn comes from the German "Ich bring dir" or "Bring's dir." Ariosto also mentions this as a non-Italian custom in his *Satire* (no. 2), using it as an excuse for not being able to go to Hungary with the Cardinal Ippolito d'Este, in whose retinue he was.

And they greatly praise some man by the name of Socrates who lived at that time because he lasted through an entire night, from dusk to dawn, drinking challenges with another good man who was called Aristophanes. The following morning, as dawn broke, he discussed and resolved a difficult geometrical problem without committing any errors,[118] which showed very well that the wine had not affected him. Learned men further claim that just as risking one's life many times makes a man fearless and sure of himself, so becoming accustomed to the dangers of intemperance makes a man sober and polite. Since drinking wine as a contest in great quantities and to excess in that manner is a great challenge to the strength of the drinker, they claim that it should be done as a test of our fortitude and to accustom ourselves to resisting and overcoming the strongest temptations. Nevertheless, I think the contrary and I consider their reasons to be quite frivolous.

We find that learned men, through their grandiose talk, very often manage to have the wrong side win and reason lose. Thus we do not trust them in this matter; it could even be that they want to excuse and cover in this fashion the sins of their nation corrupted by this vice. For it could have appeared dangerous to reprimand their fellows and perhaps they feared that they should suffer the same fate as Socrates, who used to go about pointing out everybody's faults. For this reason he was accused out of envy of many heresies and other vile sins, for which he was condemned to death, even though the charges were false and he was in fact, according to their false idolatries, a good man and a Catholic.[119] It is certain, however, that he does not merit

---

[118]In the *Symposium*, Socrates discusses literary matters, not geometry. He discusses geometry in the *Meno*, but he does not drink there. This confusion of sources may be intended to be an error of the *idiota*. Socrates was born near Athens in 469 B.C. As a youth he fought courageously for Athens, but subsequently avoided public office and responsibility whenever possible. When given a position of influence, he used it to speak for justice and truth, despite the popular passions and political realities of the day. Della Casa is referring to Socrates' habit of going about deflating and refuting the reputations of his fellow citizens who were respected for their wisdom and virtue. This practice, together with his unpopular political statements regarding Athenian democracy, led to his being charged in 399 B.C. with corrupting the youth of Athens, for which he was convicted and sentenced to death.

[119]The narrator uses the word "Catholic" to refer to someone who adheres to

any praise for all the wine he drank that night, for a barrel would have drunk, or held, more. And if the wine did not bother him, this was due more to the strength of his robust head than to the self-control of a sober man.

Whatever the ancient books may say about this, I thank God that with all the other plagues that have come to us from across the mountains, this most foul one of enjoying the act of getting drunk not only as a sport but also as a glory has not yet reached us. Nor will I ever believe that temperance should ever be learned from such teachers as wine and drunkenness.

The chief steward must not invite strangers on his own nor ask them to stay for dinner with his master. No shrewd man will sit at the table on a servant's invitation. Servants, however, are sometimes so presumptuous that they appropriate their master's prerogatives. I say these things at this point more in passing than out of respect for the order I established at the beginning.

[30]

One should not take off his clothes, and especially not his lower garments, in public, that is, in the presence of decent people, because the act is not fitting to the circumstance. It could happen that those parts of the body which are kept covered would be uncovered, much to the shame of the man himself and of anyone who sees him.

One should not comb his hair nor wash his hands in public either; for these are things to be done in one's bedroom, and not in full sight of others. The exception to this is the washing of the hands which is done before sitting down to dinner, for then it should be done in full sight of others, even if you do not need to wash them at all, so that whoever dips into the same bowl as you will be certain of your cleanliness.[120]

Similarly, one should not present himself in public with his nightcap on his head, nor do up his trousers in front of others.

---

the general religious practices of his society. The anachronism of attributing Christian beliefs to the pagan Socrates is part, again, of the persona of the uneducated narrator.

[120]It was the custom in the Renaissance to have one table setting for each two people sitting at dinner.

There are some who have the habit of occasionally twisting their mouths or their eyes, or of puffing up their cheeks and blowing out their breath, or of making such similar unpleasant acts with their faces. It is best to cease doing them completely. Once upon a time, the goddess Pallas Athena,[121] as I was once told by certain learned men, took great pleasure in playing the bagpipes, and became a master of the instrument.[122] As it happened, one day when she was playing for fun near a fountain she looked into the water and, noticing the strange motions she was obliged to perform with her face in order to play the instrument, she was embarrassed and threw away the bagpipe. She truly did the right thing, for it is not an instrument for women, and in fact it is equally unsuitable for men, unless they be of such low rank that they do it professionally and for payment.[123]

What I say about unpleasant facial contortions is similarly appropriate for all the parts of the body. It is not proper either to show one's tongue, or stroke one's beard too much (as many are in the habit of doing), or rub one's hands together, or sigh, or lament, or tremble, or shake (which is what some people do), or stretch, and while stretching call out with pleasure, "Goodness me" like a peasant waking up in a haystack.

Whoever makes a noise with his mouth to indicate astonishment, or sometimes, disapproval imitates a foul thing, as you can see. Imitations are not far from the real thing.

One should not laugh in a foolish manner, nor in a gross or unseemly way, nor laugh out of habit rather than need. And I do not want you to laugh at your own jokes, for it is a type of self-praise. It is

---

[121] In Greek mythology Pallas Athena (the Roman Minerva) emerged fully formed from the head of her father, Zeus. She was the protector of Athens, goddess of arts and handicrafts, and was associated with wisdom. As Della Casa implies, she was also one of the inventors of the flute.

[122] In *Metamorphoses* VI, 382, and *Fasti* VI, 703, Ovid says that Minerva played a tibia (flute). See also Aristotle in the *Politics* and Castiglione in the *Courtier* Bk II. The instrument is changed by the uneducated narrator into a bagpipe to illustrate, again, his lack of precise literary knowledge.

[123] Although music was seen by most humanist educators to be an important part of a gentleman's education, it was to be taught as a leisure activity only. Extreme proficiency was to be avoided because others might mistake the gentleman for a professional musician and hence someone of low birth. Similarly, stringed instruments were preferred to wind instruments because of the very reason

the hearer who should laugh, not the speaker. I do not want you to convince yourself that because each one of these things represents only a small error they are, all together, equally a small thing. In fact, out of many little mistakes one big error is made, as I said at the beginning. The smaller they are, the closer others will scrutinize them, for they are not easily seen and they sneak into our habits without our noticing them. Just as continual small expenses quietly consume our wealth, so these small sins stealthily undermine, with their multitude and number, our fine and good manners. For this reason one should not take them lightly.

One should also pay attention to how one moves the body especially when speaking, for it often happens that one is so concerned with what he is saying that he does not care for anything else. There are some who shake their heads, and some who stare wildly into space, and some who raise one eyebrow to the middle of their forehead while they lower the other to their chin, and some twist their mouths, and some others spray spittle on the clothes and on the faces of the people with whom they are talking. You will also find some who move their hands so that it looks as if they want to shoo away flies from you. All these are unpleasant and unsuitable mannerisms.

I once heard it said (for as you know I have very much frequented learned men) that a worthy man whose name was Pindar[124] used to say that everything that had a sweet and refined taste was flavoured by the hand of grace and beauty.[125]

---

identified by Della Casa: the unpleasant facial gestures required to play them. Also, it was more suitable for gentlemen to perform solo rather than in ensemble work. See W.H. Woodward, *Vittorino da Feltre and Other Humanist Educators* (New York: Columbia University Teachers' College, 1963), 240–1; Castiglione, *The Book of the Courtier* (Penguin translation), Bk 2, p. 121.

[124]Pindar, the greatest lyric poet of ancient Greece, was born at Thebes in 522 B.C. and died in 442 B.C.

[125]In the opening verses to his fourteenth Olympian ode, "For Asopichus of Orchomenus, winner in the boys' short footrace," Pindar calls upon the graces saying: "Ye Graces of fertile Orchomenus, ye queens of song that keep watch over the ancient Minyae, listen to my prayer! For, by your aid, all things pleasant and sweet are accomplished for mortals, if any man be skilled in song, or be fair to look upon, or hath won renown." *The Odes of Pindar*, trans. Sir John Sandys, Loeb Classical Library (London: William Heinemann, 1919), 147.

What must I now say about those people who leave their desks and go about with a pen behind their ears? And of those who dangle their handkerchiefs from their mouths? And of those who put one of their legs on the table? And of those who spit on their hands? And of many other innumerable stupid things, which cannot all be listed, nor am I about to try. Indeed, there may perhaps be many people who will say that the very ones I have already mentioned are too many.

Publications of the
Centre for Reformation and Renaissance Studies

Occasional Publications

Humanist Editions of the Classics at the CRRS. Comp. N.L. Adamson et al. (1979), pp. ix, 71.

Humanist Editions of Statutes and Histories at the CRRS. Comp. K. Eisenbichler et al. (1980), pp. xxi, 63.

Bibles, Theological Treatises and Other Religious Literature, 1492-1700, at the CRRS. Comp. K. Eisenbichler et al. (1981), pp. 94.

Published Books (1499-1700) on Science, Medicine and Natural History at the CRRS. Comp. W.R. Bowen and K. Eisenbichler (1985), pp. ix, 35.

Language and Literature. Early Printed Books at the CRRS. Comp. W.R. Bowen and K. Eisenbichler (1986), pp. ix, 112.

Register of Sermons Preached at Paul's Cross (1534-1642). Comp. M. MacLure. Revised by P. Pauls and J.C. Boswell (1989), pp. 151.

Annotated Catalogue of Early Editions of Erasmus at the CRRS. Comp. E. Rummel and J. Glomski (forthcoming).

Renaissance and Reformation Texts in Translation

Lorenzo Valla, *The Profession of the Religious* and the principal arguments from *The Falsely-Believed and Forged Donation of Constantine.* Trans. O. Z. Pugliese (1985), pp. 74. (2nd ed. forthcoming).

Giovanni della Casa, *Galateo.* Trans. K. Eisenbichler and K. R. Bartlett. 3rd ed. (1994), pp. 98.

Bernardino Ochino, *Seven Dialogues.* Trans. R. Belladonna (1988), pp. 96.

Nicholas of Cusa, *The Layman on Wisdom and the Mind.* Trans. M.L. Führer (1989), pp. 112.

Andreas Karlstadt, Hieronymus Emser, Johannes Eck. *A Reformation Debate: Karlstadt, Emser, and Eck on Sacred Images.* Trans. B.D. Mangrum and G. Scavizzi (1991), pp. 115.

Whether Secular Government Has the Right to Wield the Sword in Matters of Faith: A Controversy in Nürnberg in 1530. Trans. J.M. Estes (forthcoming).

For additional information, contact:
CRRS Publications, Victoria University, Toronto M5S 1K7
(416) 585-4484   fax: (416) 585-4591   e-mail: crrs@epas.utoronto.ca